Web Site Design

FOR PROFESSIONAL PHOTOGRAPHERS

Step-by-Step Techniques for
Designing and Maintaining a
Successful Web Site

**Paul Rose and
Jean Holland-Rose**

AMHERST MEDIA, INC. ■ BUFFALO, NY

Front cover photo by J.R. Sterling of J.R. Sterling Fine Art Photography (www.sterlingphotography.com). Hair and makeup by Kari Larsen of About Face Design Team (www.bridalbeauty.com).

Photographs by Karen Ault, Wes Ault, Richard Cyril Coad, Wayne Ebinger, Rick Ferro, Deborah Lynn Ferro, Gary Fox, Wayne Lukens, Rhett Pyle, Guillermo Rodriguez, Derek Smith, J. R. Sterling and Robert Tancott

Published by:
Amherst Media, Inc.
P.O. Box 586
Buffalo, N.Y. 14226
Fax: 716-874-4508
www.AmherstMedia.com

Publisher: Craig Alesse
Senior Editor/Production Manager: Michelle Perkins
Assistant Editor: Barbara A. Lynch-Johnt

ISBN: 1-58428-097-2
Library of Congress Card Catalog Number: 2002113005

Printed in Korea.
10 9 8 7 6 5 4 3 2 1

Notice of Disclaimer: The information contained in this book is based on the author's experience and opinions. The author and publisher will not be held liable for the use or misuse of the information in this book.

table of contents

about the authors

Paul Brooks Rose and Jean Holland-Rose have been designing, hosting and maintaining successful photography and small business sites for the past ten years in Central Florida, an area fast becoming a premier wedding destination. As a team, they are the powerful sales and marketing force behind the web sites of many top wedding professionals in the area. One of their projects, master photographer Rick Ferro's web site, was nominated this year by "Photography Masters" as the most user-friendly site in Central Florida.

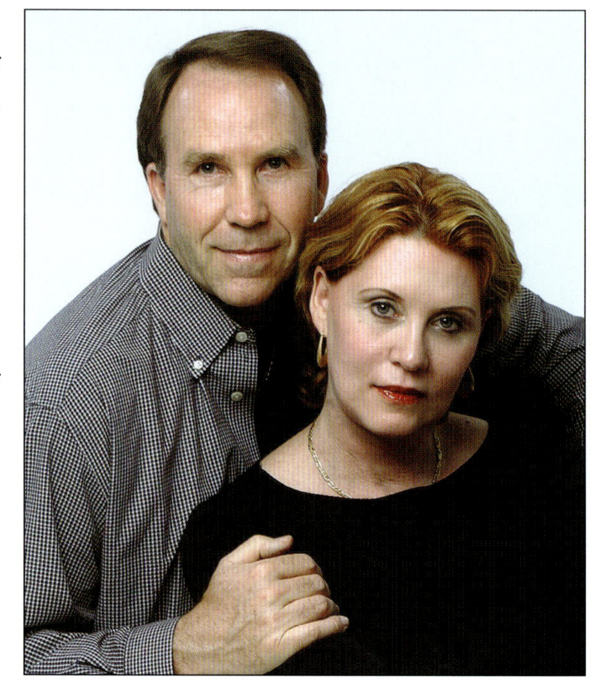

Photo by J.R. Sterling.

Paul Brooks Rose is from Salt Lake City, Utah where he earned his Bachelor of Science degree in Chemical Engineering from the University of Utah. His course of study also included programming languages and computers. This background provided a natural progression into programming JavaScript, HTML, and other Internet programming languages as well as using the latest software for image processing and web-page design. His most sought after expertise continues to be his search-engine strategies using the latest Internet technology behind the scenes. Paul's artistic flair for web design is seen throughout his work and his Photoshop skills are cutting edge. Featured as a guest speaker at a recent WPPI (Wedding and Portrait Photographers International) convention, Paul presented a program to photographers around the globe on web site tools and Internet strategies.

Jean Holland-Rose is an experienced and powerful motivator and marketing strategist, having many years of experience in the field of public relations, marketing and sales. As Marketing and Public Relations Director for Orlando Web Site Design, she is responsible for working with each web site client to ensure that each site is both user friendly and contains the necessary elements for attracting and keeping visitors' interest, thus promoting the client's success on the World Wide Web. She has won many awards in the field of sales and marketing and has been key in creating award-winning advertising slogans throughout the wedding professional industry.

The authors welcome questions and concerns regarding web site design and marketing strategy, and are also available for speaking engagements and web site forums. They can be reached at book@hollandrose.com.

acknowledgments

A thank-you to master photographer Rick Ferro and wife Deborah Lynn of Signature Studio, for the use of the beautiful images from Rick's master-class presentation as well as for Deborah's high-fashion photo contribution. Thanks, Rick, for believing in us. We treasure your friendship and special zest for life.

To each of our wonderful Central Florida photographers, our friends and web site clients, who contributed their amazing images to this, our first publication. We salute all of you for your commitment to excellence and dedication to your art.

To our children: Leave a footprint you can be proud of for others to follow. Enjoy each day and strive to become the best at each endeavor. Never stop learning. Our love to all of you!

A special acknowledgement to Tim Herring who encouraged us to create our first web site and has been a wonderful friend and confidant. To our friend, Mike Himmelstein, computer programmer, thanks for inspiring us to go the limit.

Last but certainly not least, we owe a great debt of gratitude to our publisher Craig Alesse and our editor Michelle Perkins of Amherst Media for taking on the challenge.

introduction

GOALS

Our primary motivation for writing this book was, of course, to share our experience and knowledge of web design and Internet strategies with as many readers as could be reached. Our discovery that there were very few (if any) books like this one being written for professional photographers, and understanding the usefulness of this reference material provided additional motivation.

We are convinced that the photography community will be well served by this book. Each reader will enjoy a higher monetary success by reaching more potential clients, while at the same time gaining notoriety among their peers by showcasing their finest images using the latest photo display techniques. After all, a well-designed web site that is also user friendly is fast becoming photographers' most important marketing tool for success.

A well-designed web site is fast becoming photographers' most important marketing tool for success.

With the advent of digital media, the home computer has deeply impacted the photography industry. More and more clients are relying heavily on the Internet to choose services. Throughout this book you'll be given tips on developing marketing and Internet strategies helping you become more "web savvy."

Many of you may already have attempted to design your own web sites as a cost-saving option. It is for you—professional photographers, the photographers of the future, and web designers for photographers who are interested in learning more about both basic and cutting-edge design—that we have created this book.

In this book, you will learn basic techniques that are easy to learn and easy to implement. You'll be shown basic, easy-to-learn

Photoshop techniques to enhance your web site or to use when designing a new site. You'll become familiar with the latest software programs for web design including Macromedia® Dreamweaver®, Microsoft® FrontPage® and Adobe® Photoshop®. With each new photo you add or delete, and with each new editing session, you will bring new and creative touches to your web site. This will insure you are competitive and staying on the cutting edge of technology.

With each new photo you add, you will bring new and creative touches to your web site.

WHAT YOU NEED

Basic Skills. To get started, you need only a few simple skills. First, you should be familiar with how to surf the Internet. You should understand the filing systems on your Windows®-based computer and how to operate Windows-based software like Microsoft Word®. It will also be useful if you possess basic skills with Photoshop. Many books are available on each of these subjects, and basic skills are all that are required to get started.

Domain Name. You will also need to have registered your desired domain name. This is accomplished by contacting a domain registrar, usually on-line. You can locate a selection of these companies by using the keywords "domain registration" in any search engine. You then select a domain name that you'd like to use and the domain registrar performs a search to determine if the name is available for use. If it is available, you pay a yearly fee to register the name for your use. The domain registrar will provide a method of control for the client, usually as a username and password.

Hosting Company. You will also need a hosting company. Hosting companies offer storage space for your web site and provide World Wide Web users access to it. There are thousands of hosting companies to choose from. Photography web sites usually contain many images that require a great deal of memory capacity, so when selecting a hosting company it is important to know how much memory they offer in each plan and whether that amount of memory is adequate for your needs. A photographer choosing to display preview albums on-line will require much more memory than a photographer with a basic web site. A basic hosting plan should have at least 200MB of memory. The hosting company should also include the following services:

E-mail account(s)

FrontPage extensions

FTP access

Reply/response form capability

Statistics gathering software

Site management control pages

For more information on this process, see chapter 6.

▶ ADDITIONAL MATERIALS

To assist you in the learning process, a selection of materials we have created is available for download on the Amherst Media web site (www.amherstmedia.com/downloads.htm). To access this download, please enter the following password: RR1756. This download includes a template that will enable you to begin creating your new web site immediately. You'll also find a gallery template. To take advantage of this template, copy the gallery folder with all its contents to your computer's hard drive. Edit the copied files with your own images while following the demonstration on pages 66–72. When finished, the files can be included in your web site as a working gallery.

1. getting started

Becoming your own site designer—or even just making changes to your existing site—may sound like a tall order. However, it is something you really can do. With a bit of practice, you'll find that building and maintaining your own web site is not only more cost-effective, but also a rewarding and challenging experience.

BECOMING YOUR OWN SITE DESIGNER

Your web site is your new storefront, no different than your office. When you meet with your clients at your business location, they are usually impressed by your finest images as they walk through the door. In the new millennium, experience is showing us that clients are increasingly relying on the Internet to choose the best of the available services. As a result, your web site is the first impression these prospective clients receive of your expertise and talent.

Clients are increasingly relying on the Internet to choose the best of the available services.

By learning site design and Internet strategy, you'll also be able to take advantage of the new tools of the industry and increase your chances for success. Because of these advantages, more and more photographers worldwide are taking a personal interest in web site design. They are taking an active role, choosing not to merely leave the decision-making in the hands of a stranger.

Once you develop a successful on-line strategy, you'll find that more and more of your income will be generated by your web site. With it, you can reach clients around the globe—not just those around the corner.

► MAKING CHANGES TO AN EXISTING WEB SITE

You will be able to update your site as often as needed without waiting for a web master . . .

We've heard so many times that "Time is money." Photographers often feel that they'd rather be involved in their craft—shooting award-winning photos and meeting with clients—than learning web design. However, we also hear from these same photographers, that it might be nice to occasionally (when the mood strikes) replace, add or delete an image—or just add some text to a few pages. When you can make your own changes to an existing web site, you will be able to update your site as often as needed without waiting for a web master who might be inundated with other web site work.

► SOFTWARE TOOLS

Let's begin by reviewing several software tools that are popular in the industry. We'll be discussing their differences and, at the end of this chapter, you'll be able to determine which software best suits your needs.

Having used all of the software listed, we recommend Microsoft FrontPage as the top choice for beginning web designers. As a photo editor, Photoshop is the industry standard and you'll find many Photoshop tips throughout the book.

Microsoft FrontPage. Microsoft FrontPage provides new users with the tools to create aesthetically pleasing and productive web sites. Our experience has shown us that it is easy to learn and user-friendly for first time web designers.

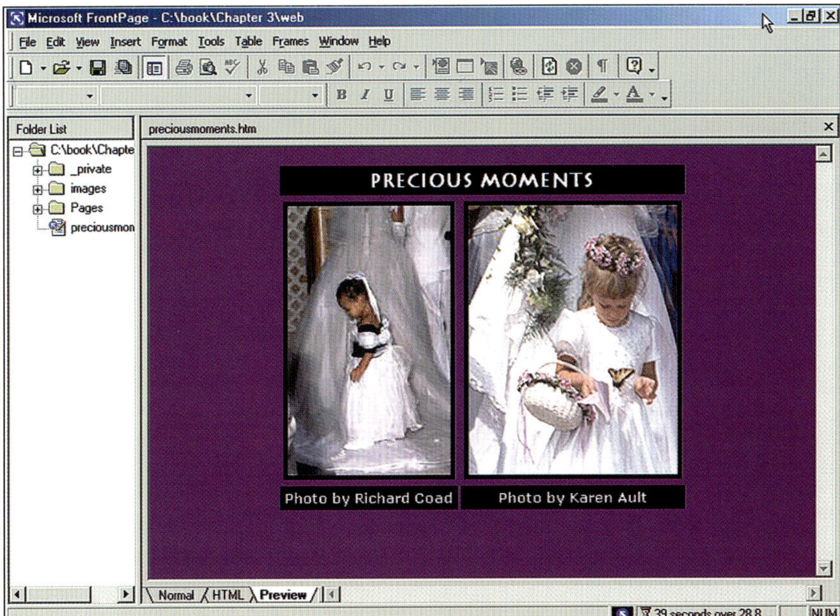

figure 1–1: FrontPage working area and filing system. Photographs by Richard Coad and Karen Ault.

FrontPage is a WYSIWYG ("What You See Is What You Get") product, meaning you don't need to learn or know any programming language. On the other hand, if you are the type who wants to write your own programs, FrontPage does also give you access to the programming source code you'll need to do this.

The ability to manage your entire web site is a key feature of FrontPage, which allows you to create web site pages and gives you the ability to view, edit, and organize all of your documents. FrontPage also has a number of features especially useful to photographers. These are located in the picture toolbar and include: brightness, contrast, thumbnail creation, cropping, sizing, rotating, borders and frames.

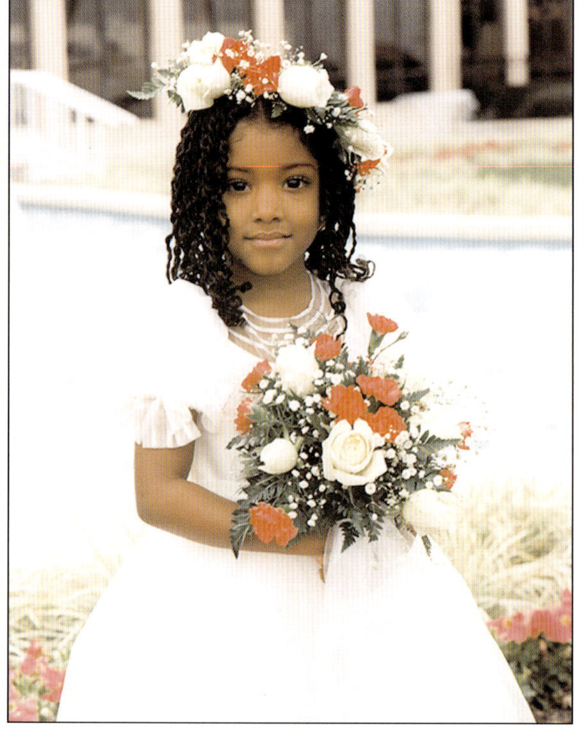

Photograph by Richard Cyril Coad.

FrontPage also comes complete with debugging capabilities for locating and correcting script errors that can cause problems and malfunctions with your web site. An additional time saving feature is the Preview, which lets you see your page as it will appear on the web without having to actually open a browser window. If you prefer to open the browser window, FrontPage gives you that option as well.

FrontPage offers over sixty templates called "themes" that allow you to create a web site using a predetermined set of images and page layout. The ability to customize these themes also allows you to take an existing layout and make it your own. This gives you ultimate control over the look and feel of your site while saving design time. You will be able to enjoy precise positioning within your document layout that can be done with both text and images using various settings within the editor portion of the program.

Microsoft FrontPage is a powerful tool and is compatible with the many browsers that clients use to view your web site—Microsoft Explorer®, AOL®, Netscape®, etc. Most, if not all, hosting companies offer Microsoft FrontPage extensions at no cost. These extensions allow you to directly access your web site from your home computer. Changes and updates are accomplished instantly without the need for secondary publishing software. (This secondary software is used for uploading web pages and is covered in chapter 7. While FrontPage allows users to connect directly to their host computer, other software requires the user to update the web pages on their personal computer, and then use the publishing software to transfer the files from their personal computer to their host computer.) With the click of a button your changes are made on-line in real time. An added feature of Microsoft FrontPage is its compatibility with other Microsoft programs like Word®, Excel®, and Access®.

Macromedia Dreamweaver. A second web page editor we'll discuss that offers full-feature capability is Dreamweaver. This software is not recommended for the beginner, but can be very useful for advanced users—especially those with experience using Flash® or Director® software since they are also by Macromedia.

One Dreamweaver feature that we especially like for photography sites is the ability to layer images one over another right in the page layout. It is possible to get the same effect using FrontPage, but the pictures need to be layered into a single composite image using Photoshop, then exported into FrontPage to be used on the web site.

Because FrontPage is not available for Macintosh, Dreamweaver is also the most common web development software used by Macintosh owners.

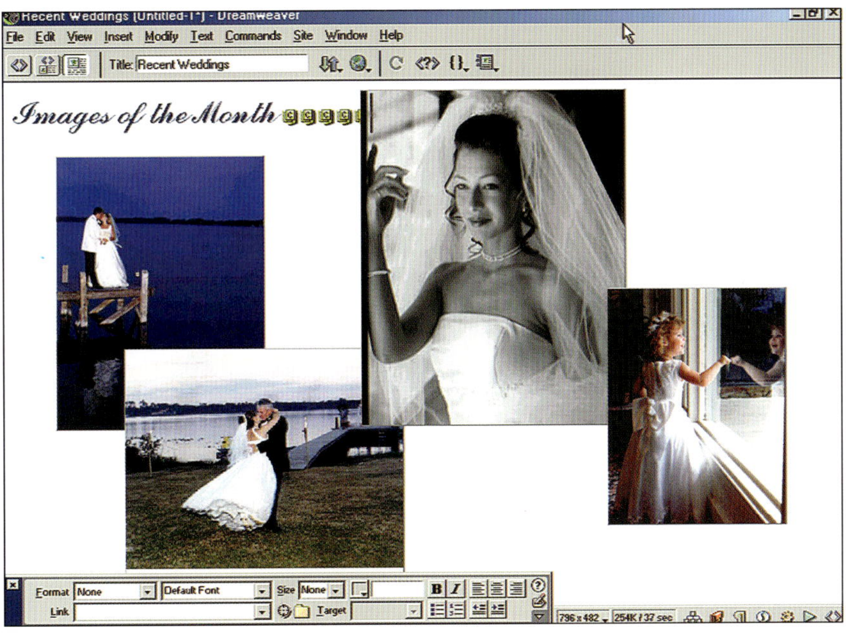

Figure 1-2: Dreamweaver page editor demonstrating layering of images. Photography by Robert Tancott.

All other design features of Dreamweaver can be accomplished more easily using FrontPage. Dreamweaver does not offer direct access to your host computer for instant edits, a big reason to use FrontPage. With Dreamweaver, you edit pages that are stored on your home computer, then transfer the pages to your host computer using an FTP (file transfer protocol) connection (see chapter 7).

Adobe Photoshop. Adobe Photoshop is the industry standard for image editing. Photoshop enables graphic artists, webmasters, and photographers to create original designs, retouch and correct

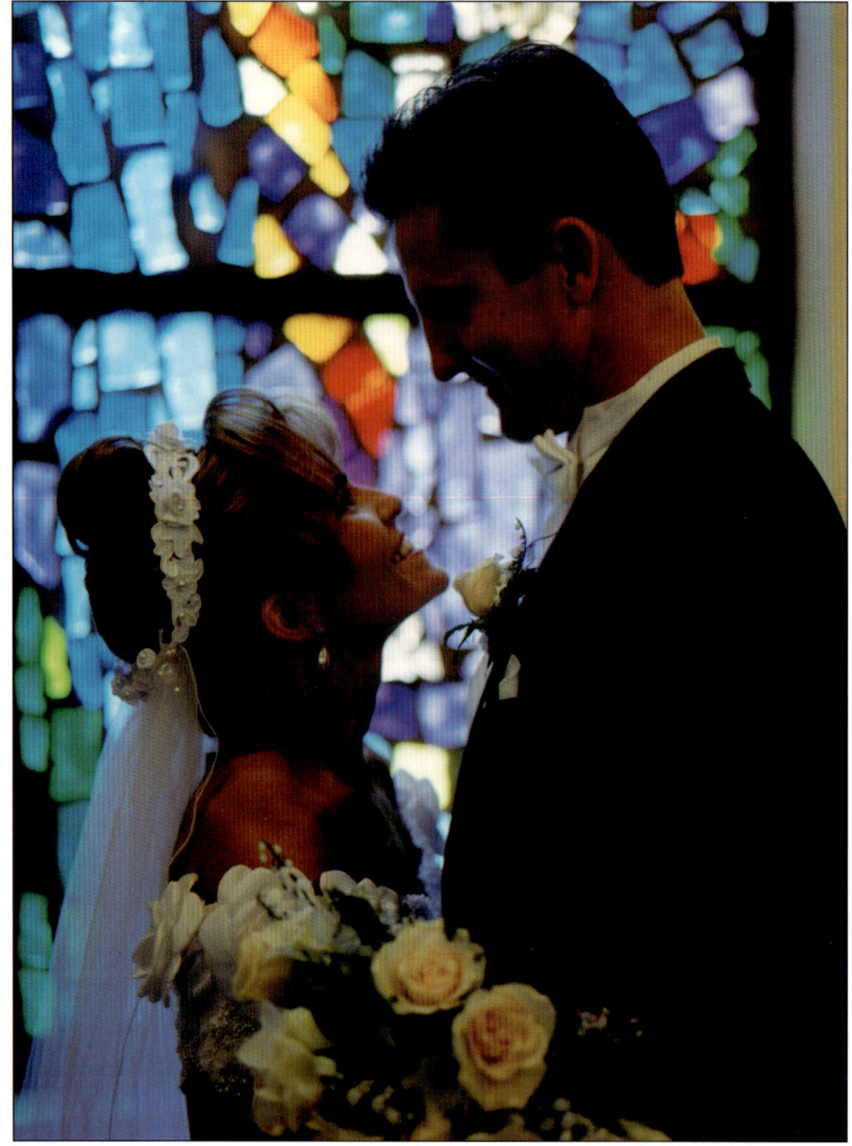

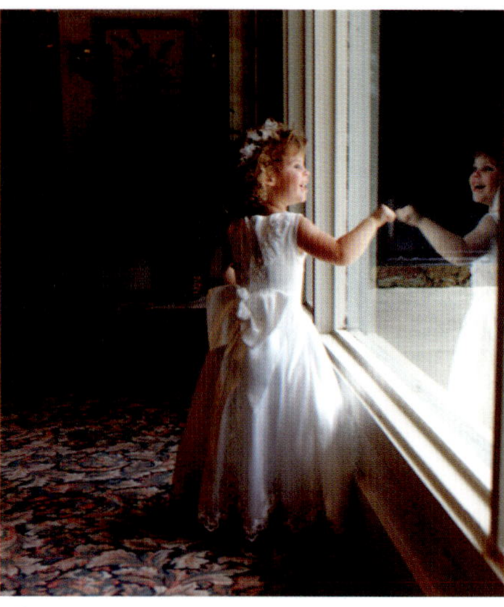

Photography by Robert Tancott.

images, and output the finished product in print or digital media. For web site design, Photoshop offers features for making buttons, logos, backgrounds, and special text. Photoshop capabilities that aid in the design of web pages will be demonstrated in chapter 3.

Photographers especially appreciate the ability created by Photoshop to clean up, correct, enhance, and retouch old and problematic images. Using this software, you can repair and restore damaged or antique photography, as well as correct common problems such as blemishes, spots, tears, color casts, exposure problems, red-eye and more. Your clients may particularly appreciate the ability to whiten teeth, smooth skin, and conceal blemishes. Photoshop allows you to correct a dark photo, a washed-out photo, and perform color corrections. You can also create dramatic color effects for high-fashion images, or soften black & white images with a sepia-tone effect.

Choose from the many tools built into the software to give your images new life.

Photoshop is a must-have for web design and for photographers using digital media to showcase their images.

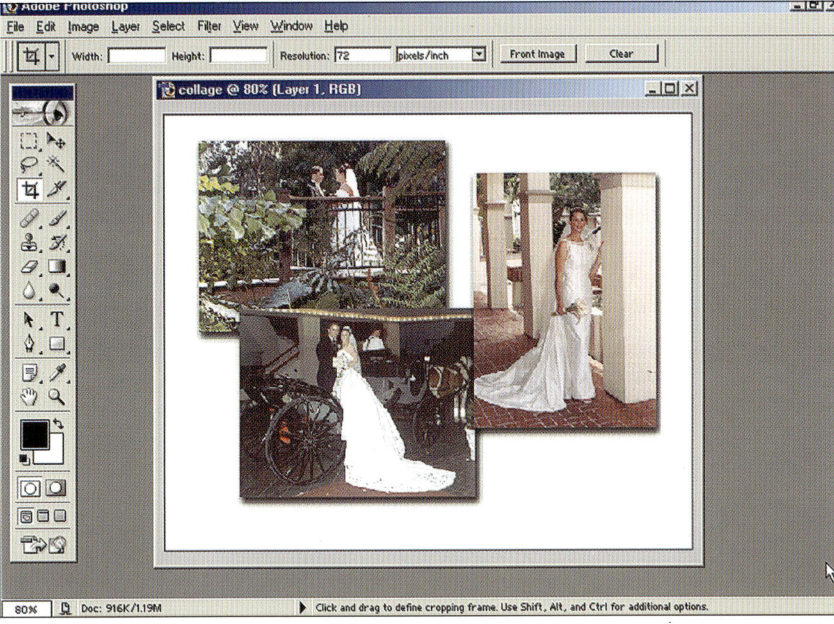

Figure 1-3: Screen shot showing layering and shadow effects using Photoshop. Photography by Wayne Lukens.

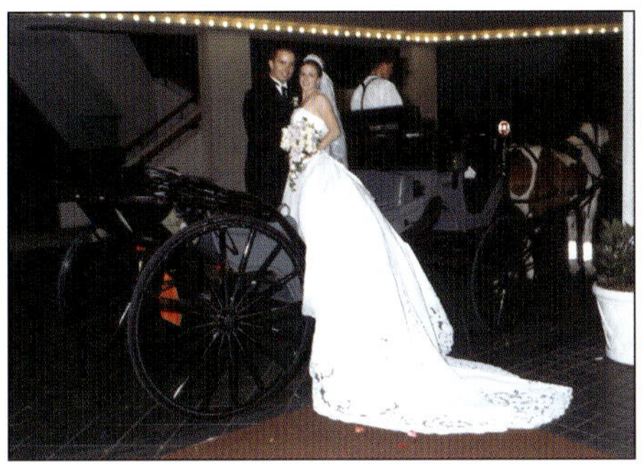

Photography by Wayne Lukens.

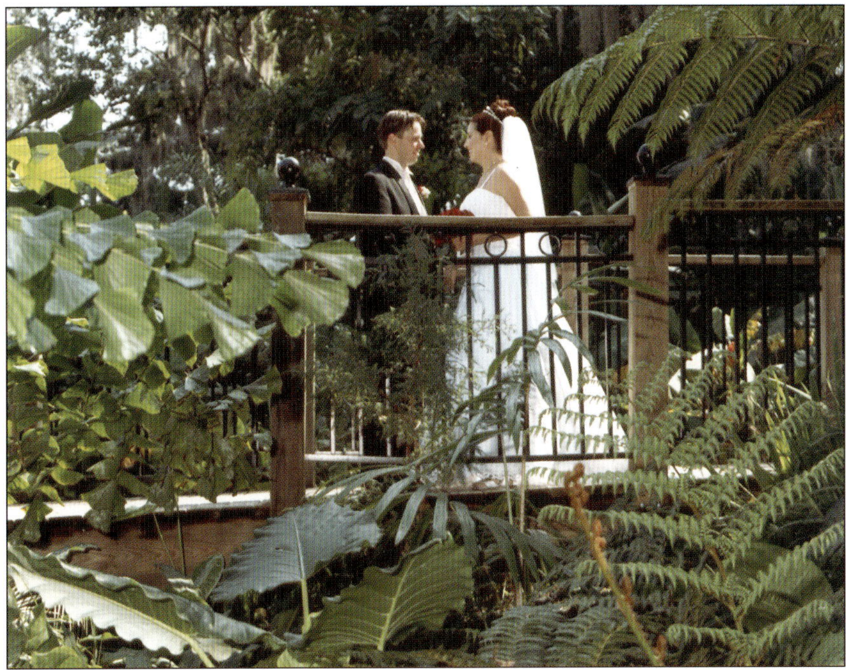

Macromedia Flash. Multimedia web presentations are made possible through Macromedia Flash software. As the name multimedia implies, Flash combines photos, sound, animation, and interactivity for a full-sensory web site experience.

The software takes advantage of MP3 format sound files and vector graphics that keep the file sizes small for quick loading over the

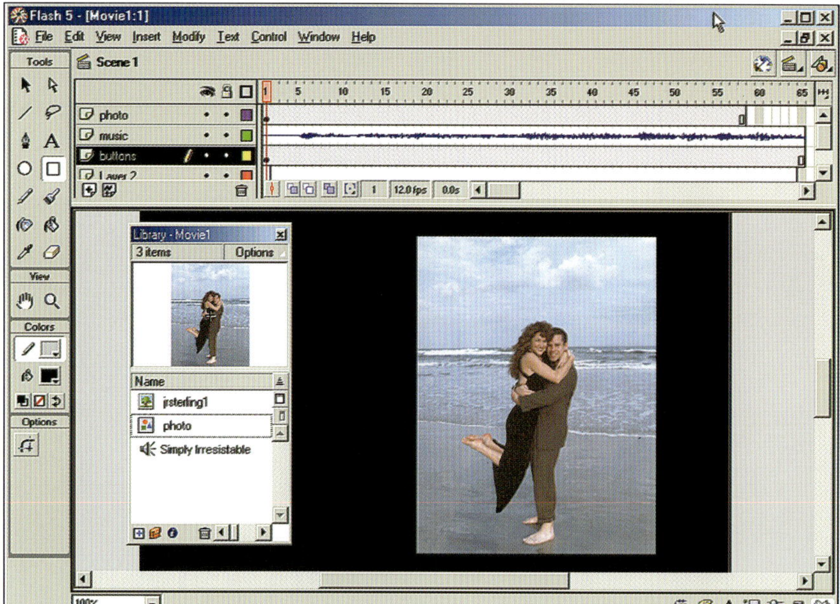

Figure 1-4: Flash software offers multimedia capability with music, sound, photos and animation. Photography by J.R. Sterling.

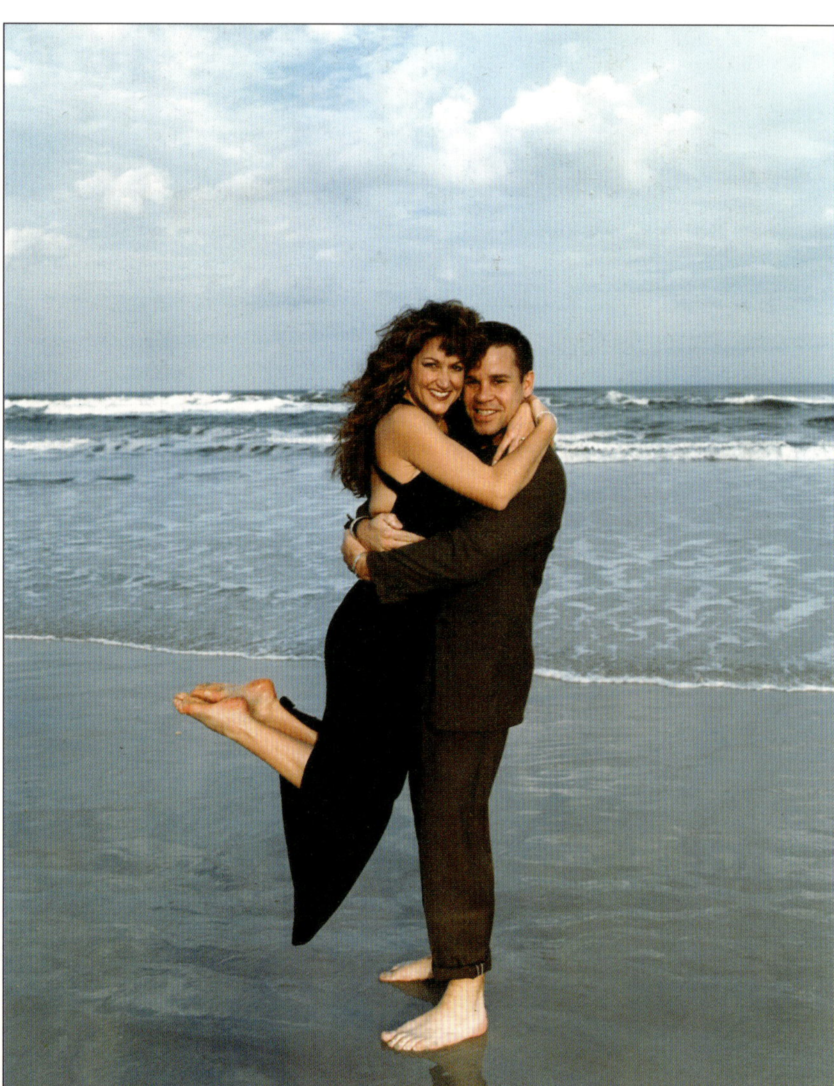

Photography by J.R. Sterling.

Flash software can be used effectively to present your images using sound, animation and interactivity.

Internet. The final factor in Flash's ability to create fast-loading multimedia presentations is the use of streaming content. Just as you read a book one page at a time, you don't need to see all pages at once, Flash programs allow the viewer to see and hear the beginning of the presentation while the balance is downloading to the browser. Prior to streaming technology the entire presentation file would need to download to the browser before viewing could occur, which would not be practical for the Web.

Flash software is not a necessity for the web site designer, but it can be used effectively to present your images using sound, animation and interactivity. Flash software is also not for the beginner. You should plan to take some classroom instruction to become an effective Flash developer, or subcontract a multimedia artist to prepare your presentation.

2. elements for success

Have you ever noticed, as you're looking for a great spot to have dinner, you are immediately drawn to the pleasing aspect of a restaurant's storefront? Most of us are attracted by color and design—and your web site background is your new "storefront." The color scheme of your site creates an impression about your products and services and is critical to your future success on the web.

BACKGROUND COLOR AND DESIGN

Choosing a Background Color. Often called "the silent sales person," color is used to communicate value, attract the client's eye, and hold interest. Color can make or break your web site. The psychological effect is immediate, as color stimulates the senses and communicates by power of suggestion. The color must work quickly to capture the client's interest in a short time. There are several "top" colors that tend to be successful choices for photography web sites. These colors are white, black, purple, green and blue. Let's touch on a few colors below and explain their powerful messages.

Color is used to communicate value, attract the client's eye, and hold interest.

RED

Excitement and high energy, dynamic and provocative, sexy

PINK

Romantic, energetic and youthful, spirited, sweet

ORANGE

Hottest of all colors, playful, gregarious, childlike, intense

BROWN

Down to earth, durability, rustic and rich

YELLOW

The splendor and heat of the sun, cheerful, warming, sunny, delicious. Used in conjunction with red to stimulate appetite.

BLUE

Dependable, cool, quiet, associated with sky and water, serene, inspires confidence making it ideal for web sites.

GREEN

Healing, freshness, soothing. Identified with money and prestige. Darker greens are excellent colors to promote a business web site.

PURPLE

Mysterious, elegant, spiritual. Very powerful when used in conjunction with black and white. Good for technology products.

WHITE

Purity, simplicity. Effective in packaging and product design. Sense of clarity and cleanliness. Works well in contrast with any color.

BLACK

Sophisticated, powerful, dramatic, classic, elegant, expensive. Black & white is the quintessential and most classic combination of strength, clarity, power and purity.

Background Selection. Selecting just the right background will make your images the focal point of your pages, aid in showing off your finest work, and make your text easy to read. Just as matting should not overpower a framed picture, the background of your web site should not detract from the presentation of your images and text.

Black is a popular choice for many photographers. It is also a good choice for displaying black & white images in a photojournalistic style. One disadvantage in choosing a black background is that white text is not as easily read on a black background as black text is on a white one. Secondly, a black background does not allow you to use shadow effects on your images. As a rule of thumb, try to keep text to a minimum on pages that use solid black as a background.

The background of your web site should not detract from the presentation of your images and text.

You can also use an image in the background. Since most computers use an 800-pixel screen width setting, your web page needs to be 800 pixels wide. The picture you select as your background will repeat itself just like tiles on a floor. The first copy is in the upper left corner of the page, and copies of the picture repeat to the right and down until the page is filled. For example, a background picture that is 400 pixels wide will have two copies across the top and then continue down as far as the page length. A background picture that is

800 pixels wide will repeat in a single column down the page. To determine or set the size of a photo you want to use in the background, see pages 39–42. To accommodate large monitor screens or screen settings greater than 800 pixels wide it is generally good practice to make your background images 1024 pixels wide (for more information on this, see chapter 3).

web page 1024 pixels wide	
original background picture	copy of background picture
copy of background picture	copy of background picture
copy of background picture	copy of background picture
copy of background picture	copy of background picture
copy of background picture	copy of background picture
copy of background picture	copy of background picture
copy of background picture	copy of background picture

Figure 2-1: A single background image repeats to fill a page.

Personalized background images can be created by using Photoshop or other software. For example, Figure 2-2 shows a background strip created in Photoshop using a green gradient on black with the addition of a narrow vertical stripe. This strip may be used in a repeating fashion to fill a complete web page. This technique of using a small file many times allows the page to load faster than would be possible if you chose a large single picture for the background of the web page. Figure 2-3 demonstrates the effect of this photo strip used on a web page.

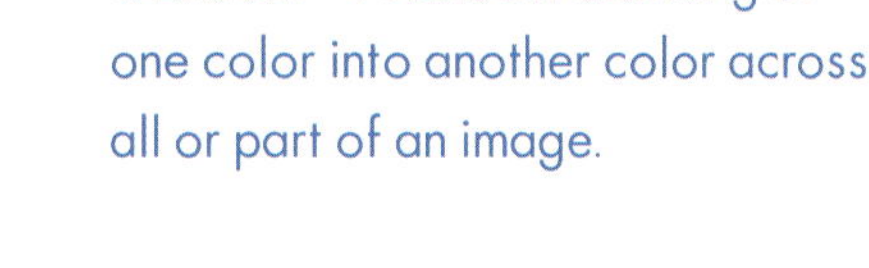
Gradient—A smooth blending of one color into another color across all or part of an image.

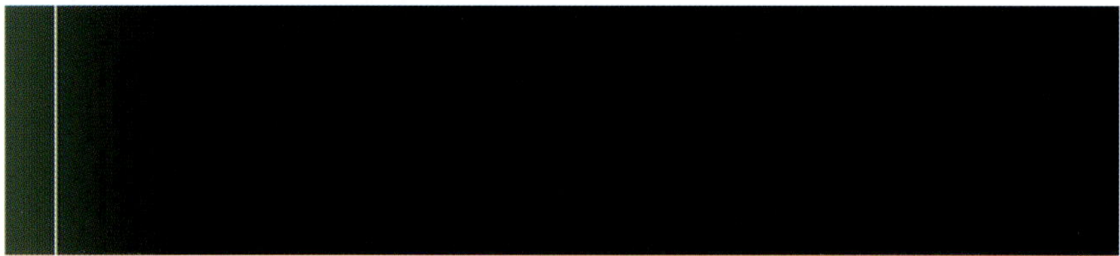

Figure 2-2: A background strip created in Photoshop.

Figure 2-3: A sample page using the background strip shown at the bottom of the facing page. Photography by Richard Coad.

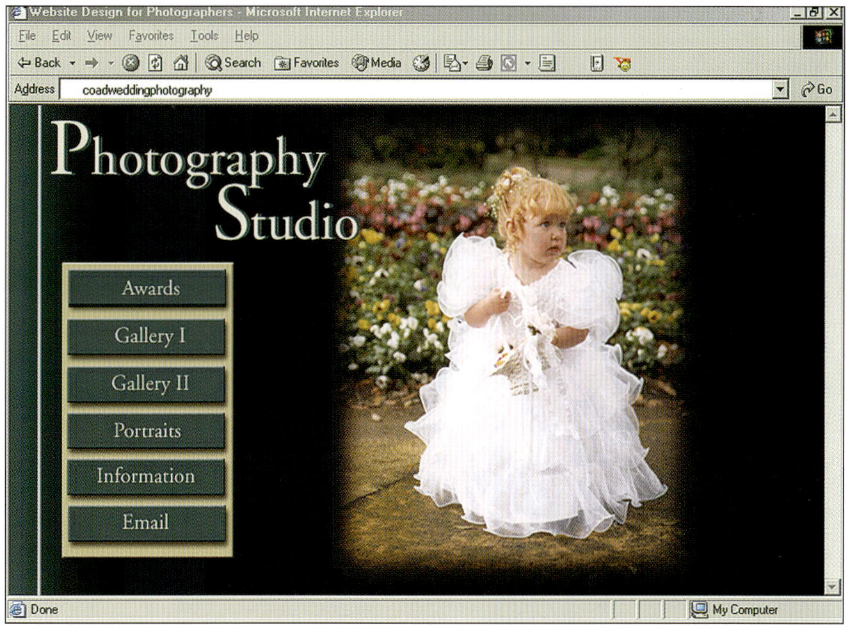

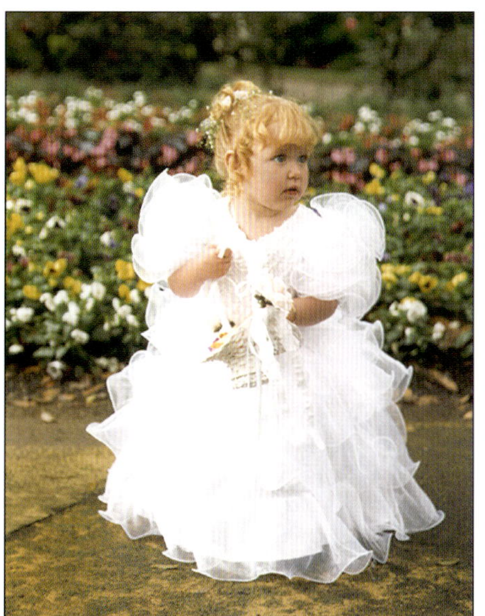

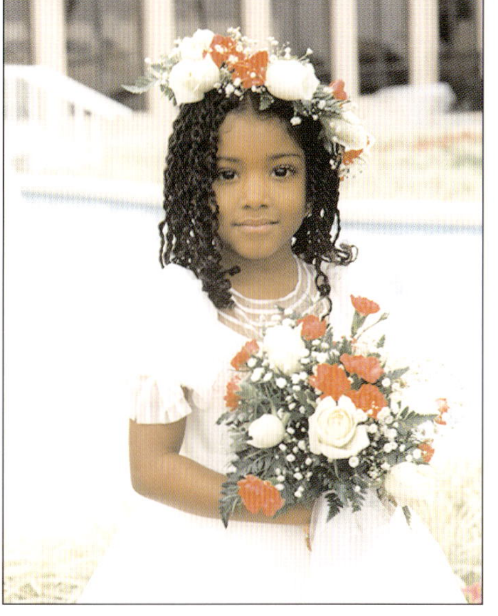

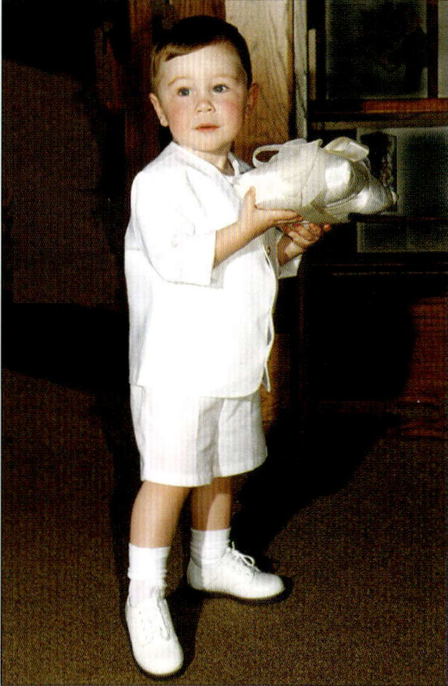

Photography by Richard Cyril Coad.

LOGO

The definition of a logo in Webster's Dictionary, "a graphic representation or symbol of a company name, trademark, abbreviation, etc., often uniquely designed for ready recognition."

Logos are used for business cards, stationary, web sites and all printed advertisements. Developing an elegant and innovative logo can enhance and promote any business to the height of success. Proper selection is critical, because logos are one of the main vehicles for communicating your company's image, as well as for gaining attention and recognition.

Some photographers already use a specific logo and find that it is working for them. This logo image should be used or given to the

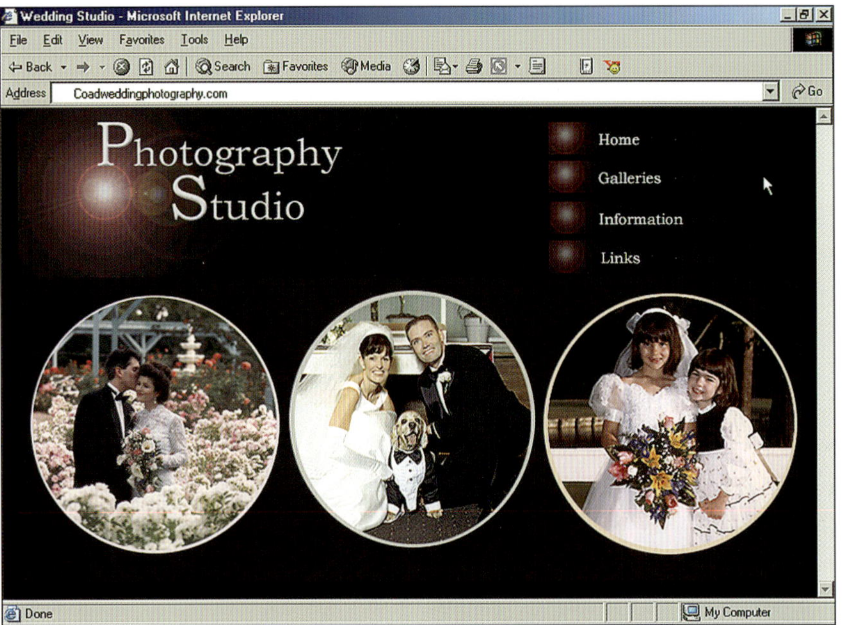

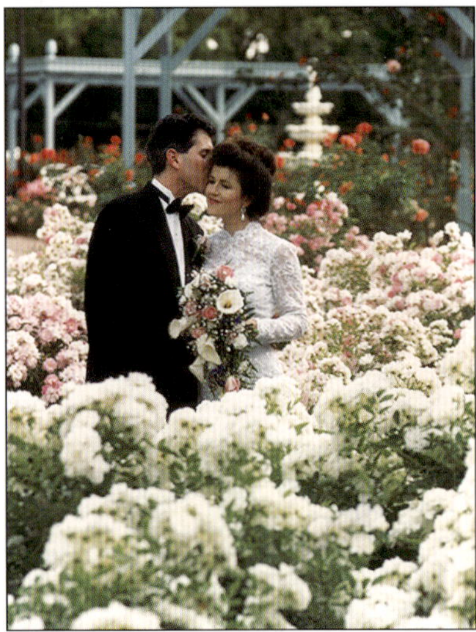

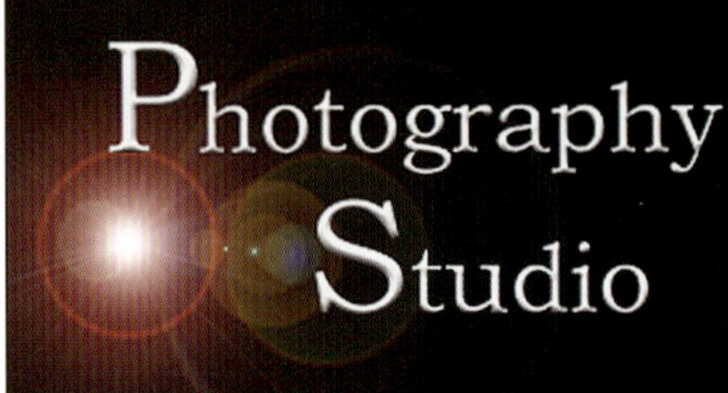

Figure 2-4 (above): Example of a logo created using Photoshop.

Figure 2-5 (top): Web page using the same logo design. Photography by Richard Cyril Coad.

Left: Photo by Richard Cyril Coad.

web designer in a clear format and should be displayed on each page of the web site. You might consider using your name (photographer's name) or company name in conjunction with a favorite image if a studio logo is not available.

You might consider using your name or company name in conjunction with a favorite image . . .

In cases of special logo requirements with complex research and design processes, the price for logo design by a graphic artist can be costly. By using Photoshop and a bit of creativity you can design your own logo as a cost-saving measure. In chapter 3, the techniques used to create the logo seen in Figure 2-4 are presented step-by-step for easy learning.

IMAGE DISPLAY

There are a myriad of techniques to display photographic images. Here are several popular choices.

Thumbnail—A miniature display of an image that can be enlarged by clicking on it.

Thumbnail. Using a thumbnail image is a popular technique. By clicking on a small thumbnail of an image, a new page opens to reveal a full-size view of that image (see Figure 2-6). This process can be time-consuming if many thumbnails are available for viewing.

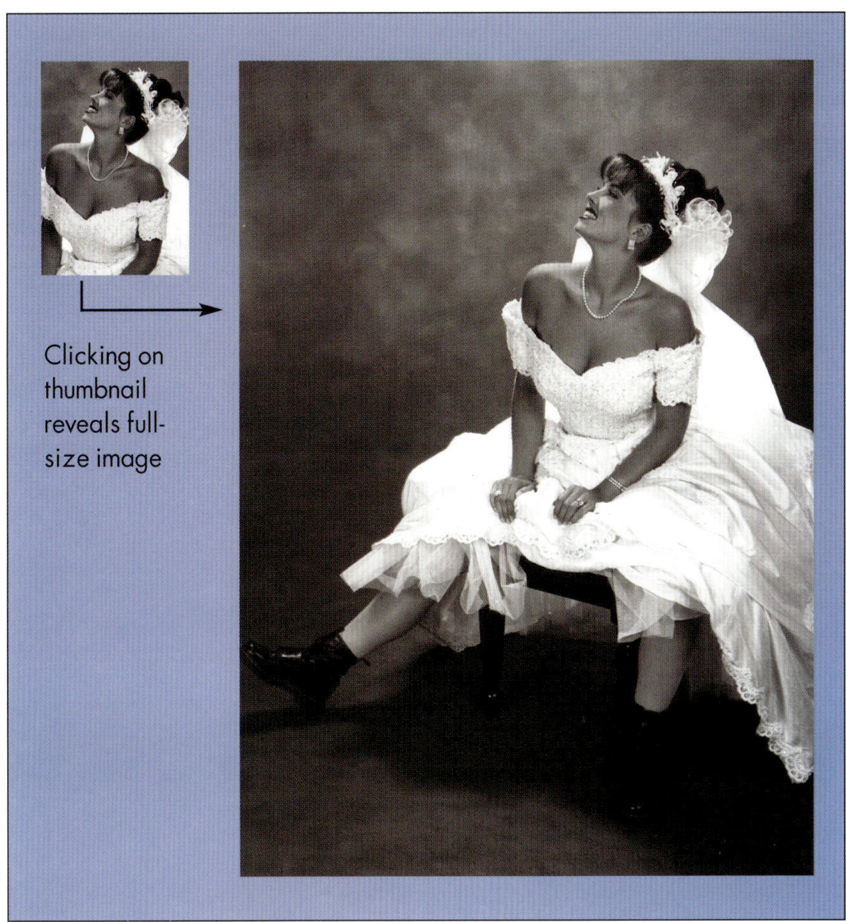

Figure 2-6: Thumbnail method for displaying images. Photograph by Richard Cyril Coad.

Many visitors prefer to see a few full-size images right away rather than look at a gallery of 15–20 images. A full-size gallery means that the pictures are already displayed in their full size. This format limits the number of images, due to space available on the web page. The advantage of this method is the viewer doesn't need to click and wait for the pictures to enlarge.

For photographers who wish to have large photo galleries, there are more user-friendly approaches for using thumbnails that eliminate the need for back-and-forth page jumping. One method, which will be demonstrated later, allows the viewer to go from a thumbnail display directly into a slide show. It is also a good idea to offer several display methods on your site for variety.

Slide Shows. As the name implies, a slide show displays images on a screen with one image following another in a sequence.

User-controlled slide shows allow the viewers to browse at their leisure, using forward and back buttons to change the pictures as shown in Figure 2-7. With the addition of user controls, viewers can pause at each image and then move on as they choose.

Automated slide shows display each image for a predefined length of time. Automated slide shows are actually JavaScript programs, Flash features, or Java Applets. A working knowledge of JavaScript, Flash, and/or HTML is required to implement the automated slide shows.

JavaScript—A computer scripting language that enables web authors to design interactive sites. Javascript can interact with HTML source code, enabling web authors to spice up their sites with dynamic content.

Java Applet—A computer application written in Java computer language. For web developers, these offer a wide range of styles and methods for displaying images and text. Java Applets may be purchased on-line and inserted into web pages to produce dynamic effects.

The JavaScript slide show simply changes pictures at a predefined time interval. A Java Applet slide show offers a bit of animation such as the pictures breaking apart and the new picture reappearing from the fragments. A Flash feature can combine a user interface with animation. For instance, it can be set up so the viewer clicks on an image, then the image changes by shrinking, growing, disappearing, etc.

A variety of slide show methods may promote visitor interest. You may decide, for example, to employ a user-controlled slide show for weddings, a JavaScript-automated slide show for portraits, and a Java Applet for photojournalism.

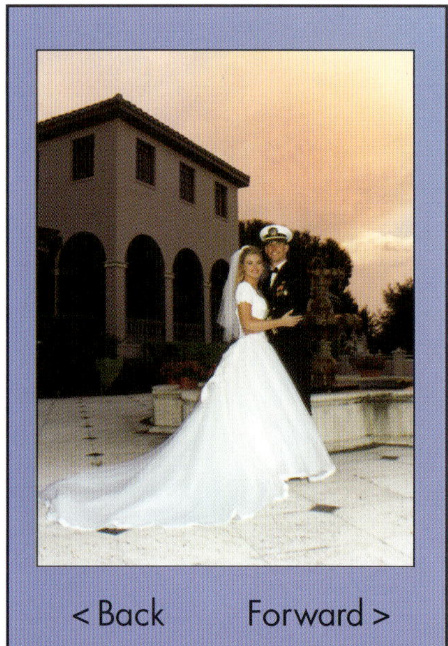

Figure 2-7: Slide-show method for displaying images. Photography by Wayne Ebinger.

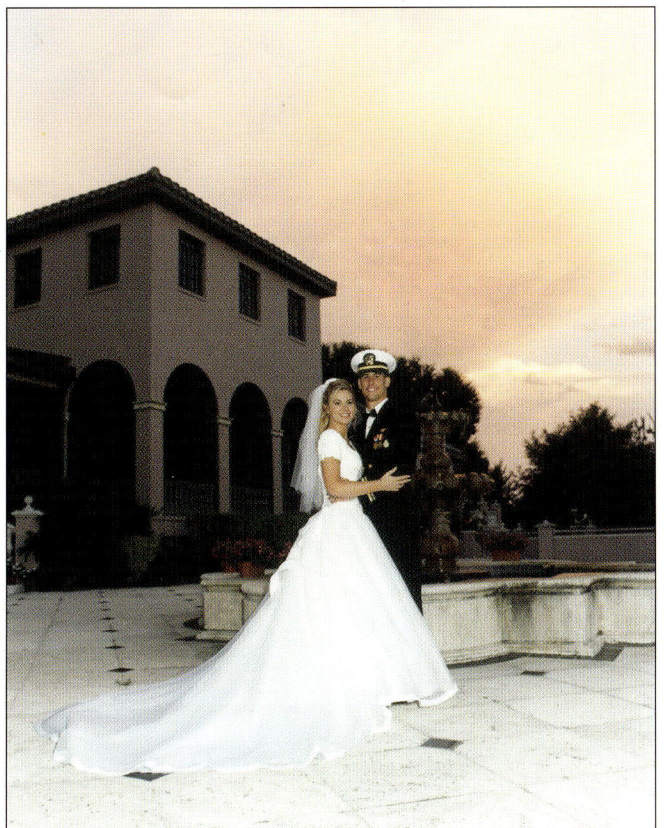

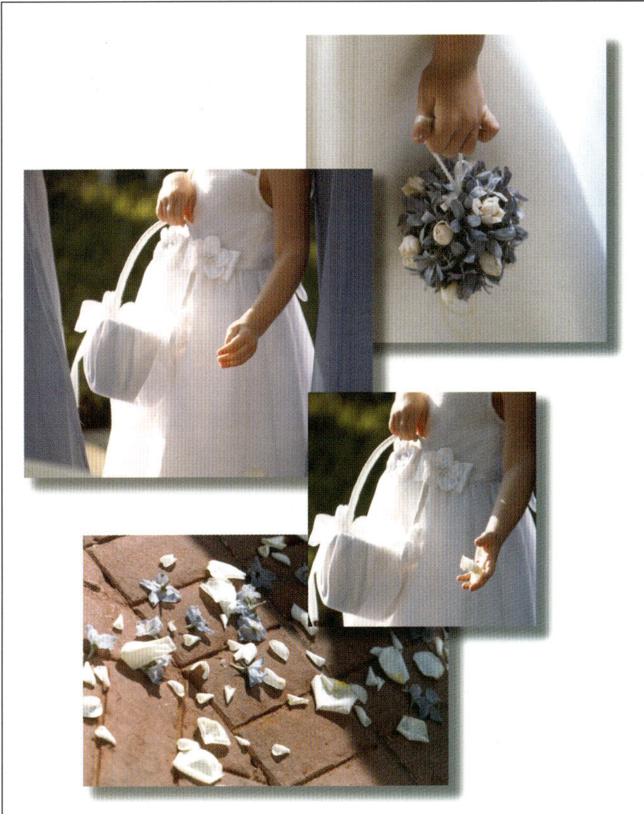

Left: Photograph by Wayne Ebinger.

Figure 2-8 (right): A photo collage features several images in a grouping. Photography by Gary Fox.

Collage. A collage is a grouping of images that are artfully displayed in a single frame. Imagine tossing a group of photos onto a table in a random fashion. The photos as a collective unit define a collage. This method is especially effective for showing off your photojournalistic images. Figure 2-8 demonstrates the storytelling effect of a collage and photojournalism.

MENU BAR

The menu bar is a navigational system (made up of hypertext links) that allows the visitor to easily go from page to page and see all of the services you offer. Viewers should be able to locate the menu bar easily on every page so they can get back to the home page and all other places of key importance. Making this something that visitors can accomplish quickly and without searching helps to create a user-friendly web site. There are many options for creating a unique menu bar.

Hyperlink—Text or a graphic containing a link to a web page. Clicking on a hyperlink connects you to the linked web page.

Plain Text Links. Plain text links, as the name implies, simply requires you to type a word or phrase and then apply a hyperlink to the text. Clicking on the text will then allow the viewer to change to another page. The default appearance for a plain text link is an underscore of the linked word or phrase. The color of the linked text may also be customized to make it stand out from the normal text of the page. You can also choose separate colors for page-links that have already been visited and those that have not.

Several methods are available to organize plain text links. One of the options is to use a table to create simulated buttons for your menu bar (as shown in Figure 2-9). The table method can be employed to create either a horizontal or a vertical look. You may adjust the color, texture, and border of the table cells. Then, simply hyperlink each new menu option (refer to chapter 5 for hyperlink instructions).

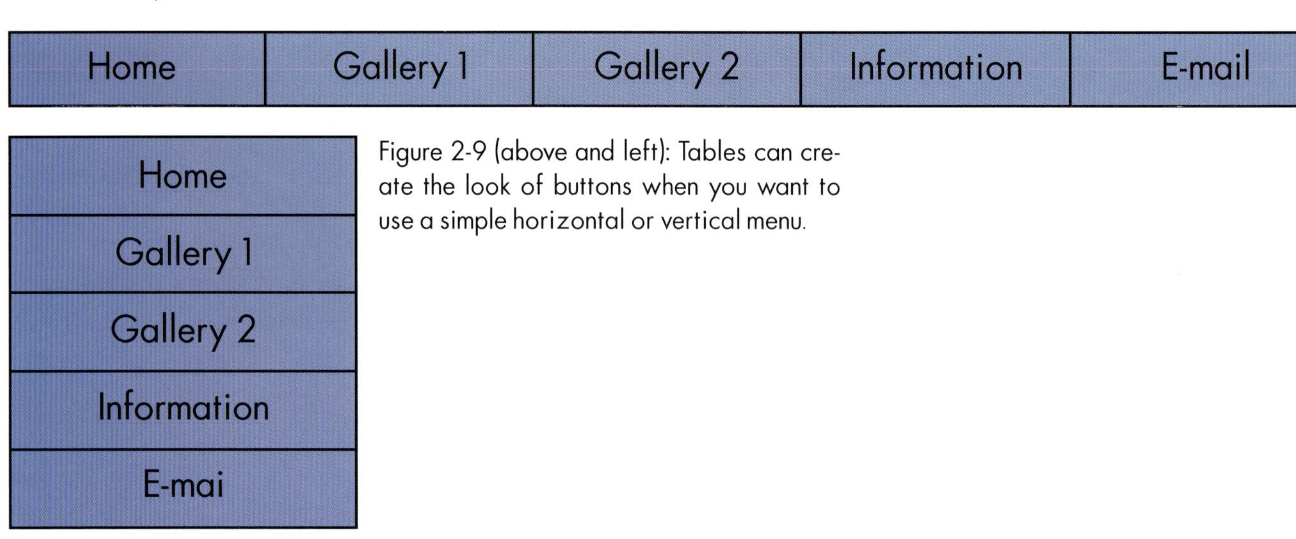

Figure 2-9 (above and left): Tables can create the look of buttons when you want to use a simple horizontal or vertical menu.

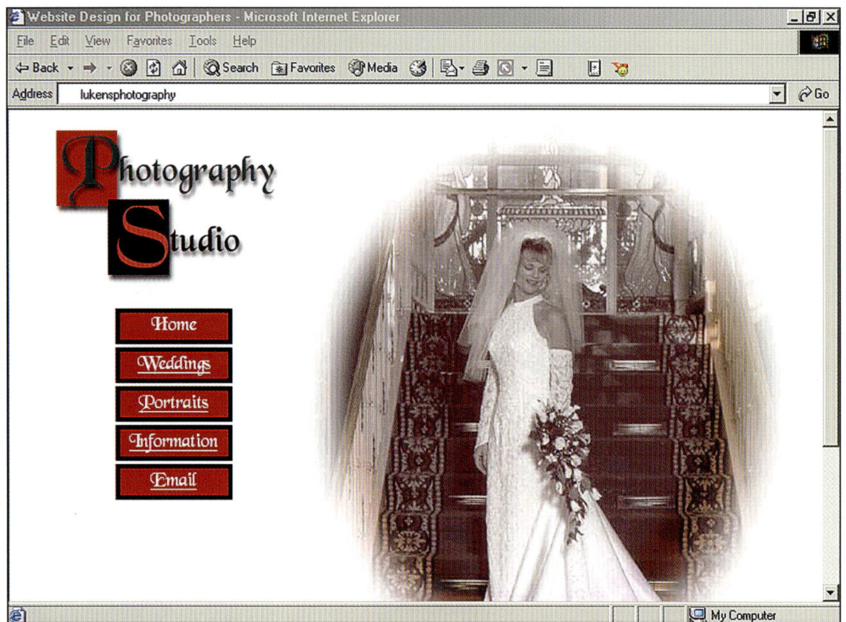

Figure 2-10: Web page using a simple vertical table as a menu. Photography by Wayne Lukens.

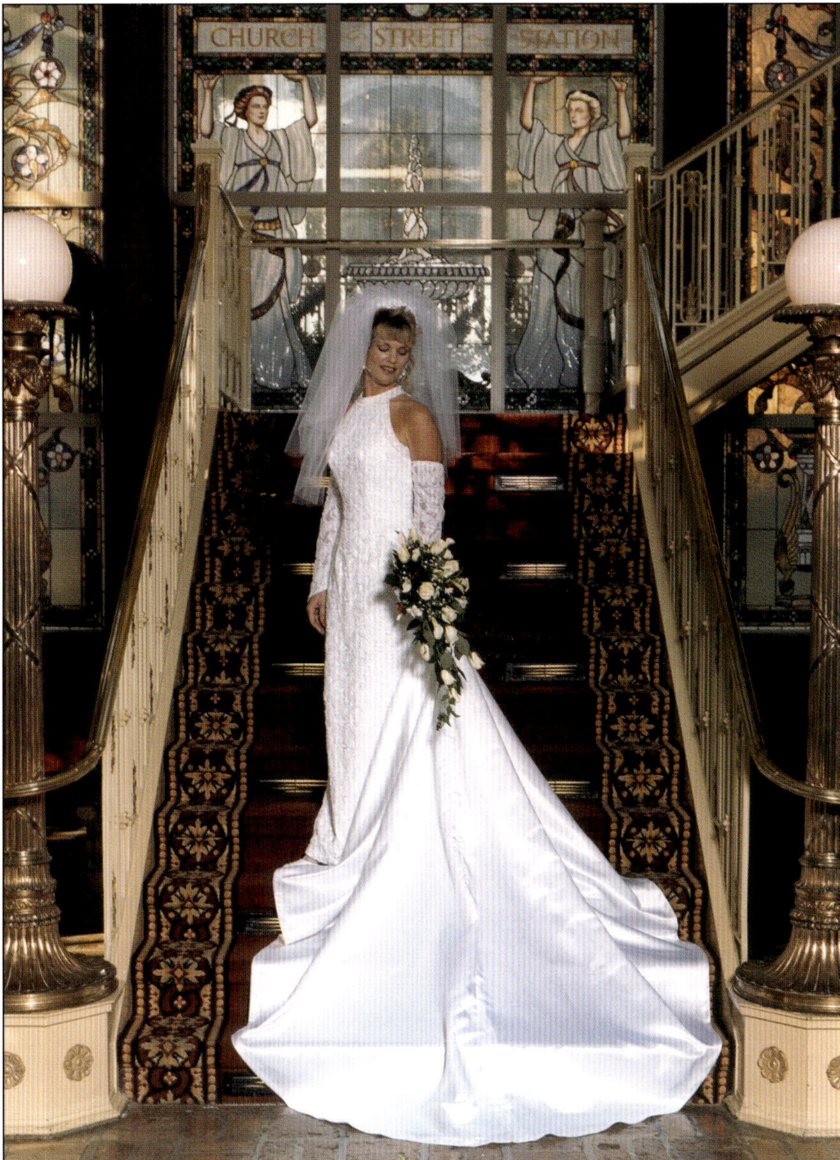

Photograph by Wayne Lukens.

A second approach for using plain text is to use bullets to offset your menu. With this method a bullet appears before each menu item (as seen in Figure 2-11).

- Home
- Gallery 1
- Gallery 2
- Information
- Email

Figure 2-11: Bullets can help to differentiate a menu from regular text. The Information link is a different color to indicate the viewer has visited it.

Backlighting Menu Bar. Backlighting is similar to a plain text link. The difference is that when the visitor's cursor points at the text, a pre-selected color appears behind the text. This feature is accomplished by using style-sheet properties. A working knowledge of style sheets is required to use this method. Several on-line tutorials are available for the interested reader. This method is very visually appealing, as it removes the underline of plain text links and permits you to choose a backlight color that compliments the color scheme you have developed for your page.

Style sheet properties—A style sheet is a file that defines the layout properties of a web page. When you fill in a style sheet, you specify such parameters as the font, background, and color scheme that will remain consistent throughout the web site.

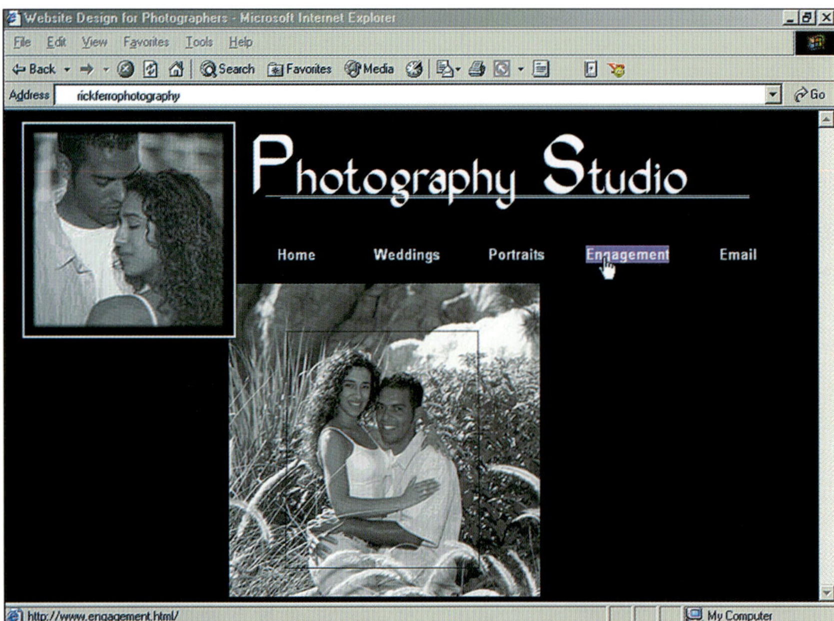

Figure 2-12: Backlighting for plain text links offers a colorful option. The link is backlit when the pointer passes over the linked text. Photography by Rick Ferro.

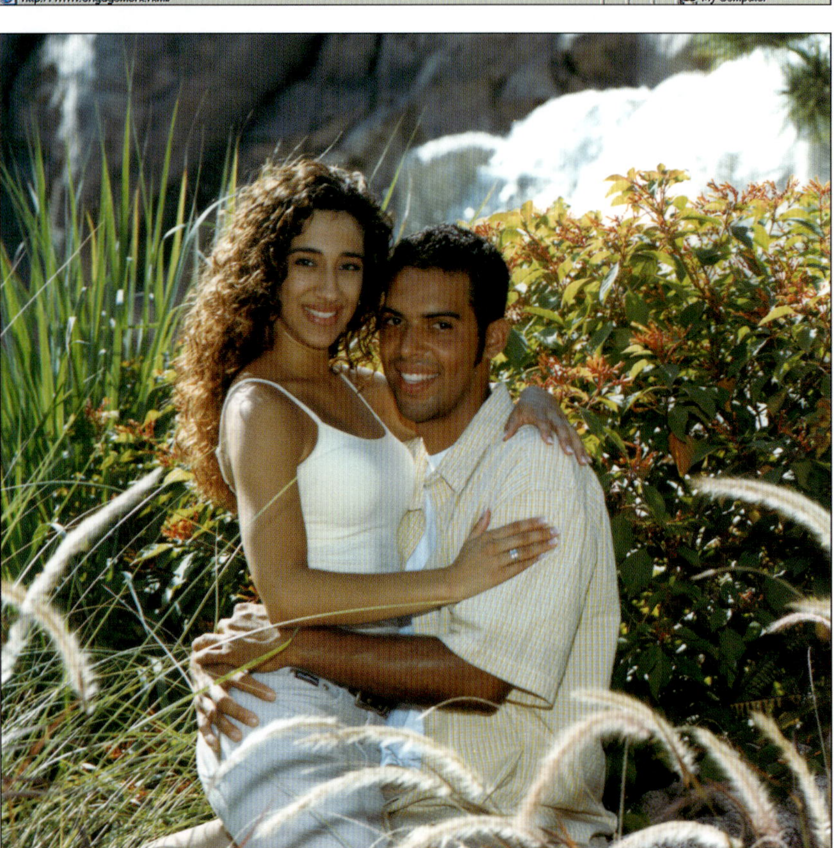

Photograph by Rick Ferro

JavaScript Button Menu. Buttons are a popular choice for many web-site menu bars and can be created in Photoshop. Chapter 3 provides the Photoshop method for making the three button styles shown in Figure 2-13. Buttons are especially useful to complement your color scheme.

JavaScript is a programming language that provides versatility to the designers of web pages. For example, a JavaScript program can use button pictures to create mouse-over effects. Such buttons are actually made up of two pictures that create the unique effect shown in Figure 2-13. When the cursor passes over the first button, the JavaScript program replaces it with the second picture, which may be a different color or offer a different text message. As a result, the button may seem to change color or employ another visual effect, or the button title may change to offer more information.

Mouse-over effects—A JavaScript element that triggers an item in a web page (usually a graphic) to change when the mouse passes over it. This usually signifies that the item is a link to related information. Widely used in navigation bars, pop-up boxes and form submissions.

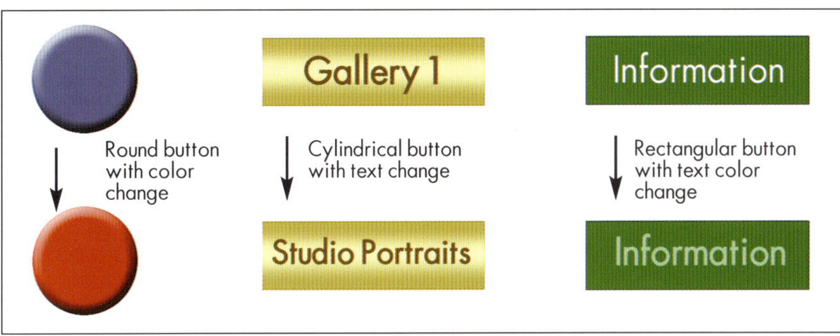

Figure 2-13: JavaScript effects using round, cylinder, or rectangular buttons.

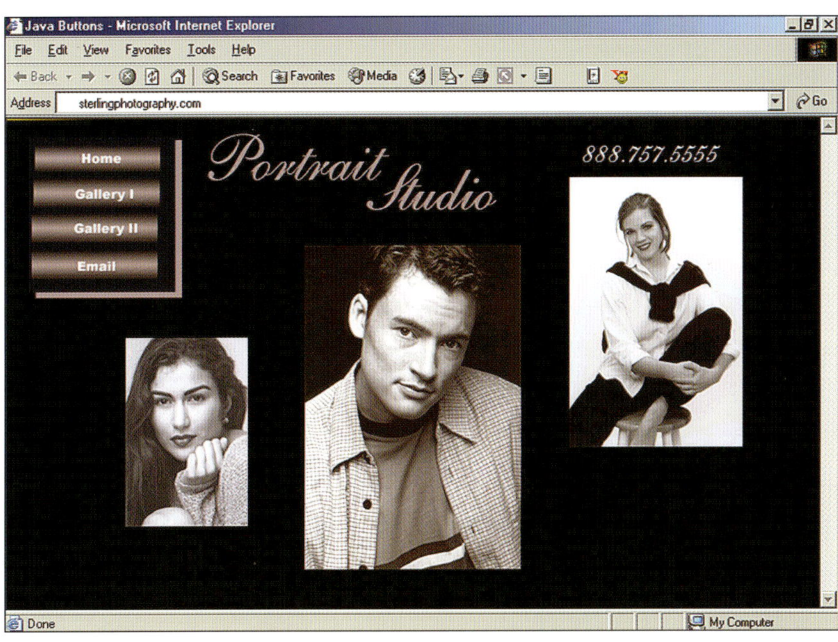

Figure 2-14: A web page using a button menu and collage image display. Photography by J.R. Sterling.

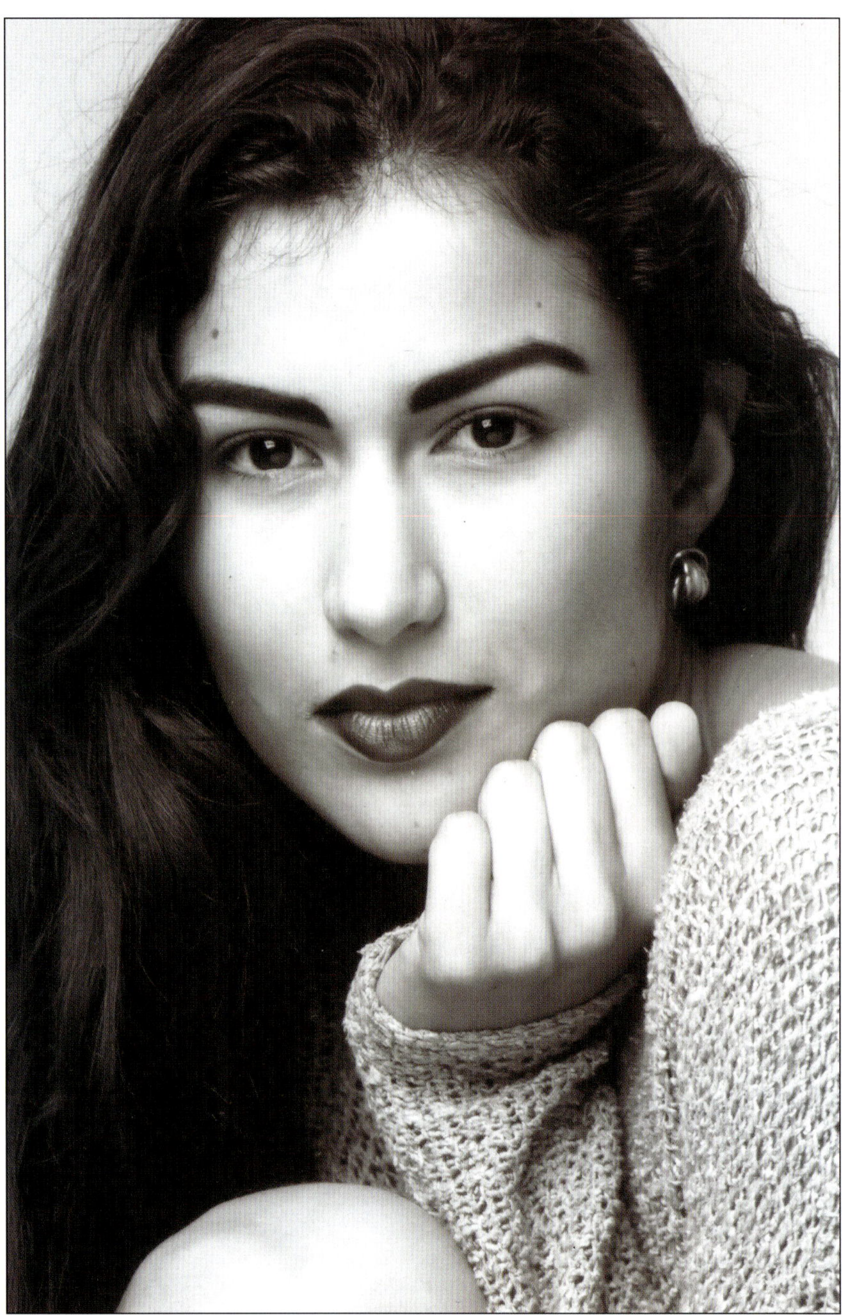

Photograph by J.R. Sterling.

DHTML Drop-down Menu. Dynamic HTML menus combine the HTML and JavaScript programming languages to make interactive menus. Although they have less animation characteristics than Flash menus, they can offer space-saving features for web sites that contain many pages or informational links. Software especially designed for creating these menus is available for on-line purchase at a minimal cost. The example below shows a single button opening a new window containing menu selections. Removing the pointer from the button closes the window again.

DHTML (Dynamic Hypertext Markup Language)—Used to create dynamic effects based on user actions. For example, a dynamic menu can be created that will reveal hidden objects when the user points at the menu.

Menu
Home
Galleries
Information
E-mail

Menu
Home
Galleries
Information
E-mail
Portrait
Wedding
Black & White
Photojournalist

Figure 2-15: A DHTML drop-down menu is a space saving device for web sites containing many pages or links. The menu will cover text or photos on the page when called into action, or disappear if not needed.

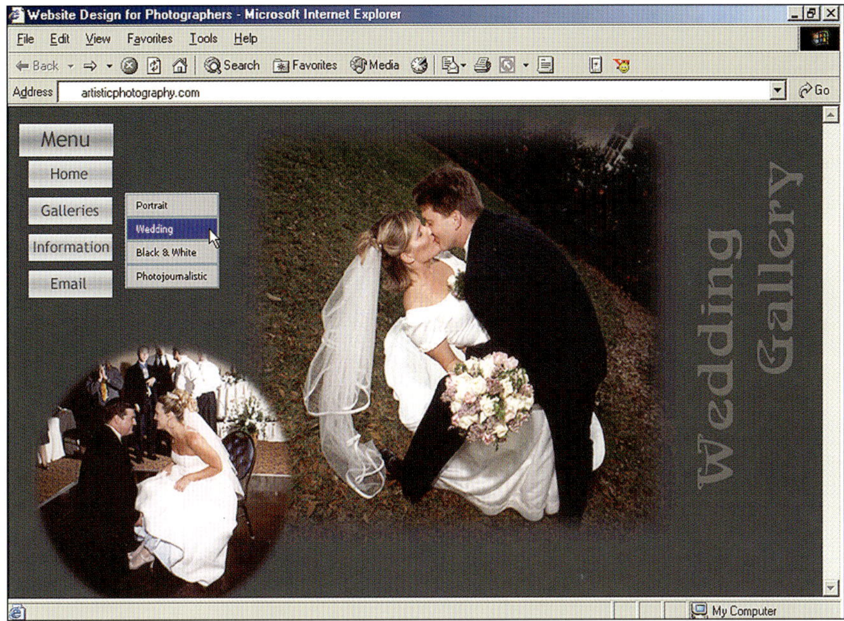

Figure 2-16: A Gallery Page demonstrating the DHTML drop-down menu fully opened. Photography by Rhett Pyle.

Flash Software Elements. A menu created using Flash software is interactive and can also include animation effects. Flash software techniques are for the more advanced web designer. If you are new to web design and want to implement Flash elements, you should consider subcontracting the task to an experienced multimedia artist. Once the Flash features are installed on your web site, they require no maintenance, therefore, for a one-time fee, you may offer your visitors Macromedia Flash animation.

INTERACTIVE ELEMENTS

Interactive features include response/reply forms, chat rooms, message boards, newsletters, bridal registries, and other pages where viewers are able to obtain information from you or provide information to you. Some photographers include a link that allows each client to build their own wedding album by viewing their wedding photos on-line. They may also be directed to a page (using a password known only to them) for private viewing of their wedding photos.

Information Form. How important is an information form (also known as a response/reply form)? It is one of the two most important pages on any photography site, second only to the home page (the first page visitors see). The response/reply form contains information fields that clients complete to let the photographer know the specifics of their events/needs. The photographer will then respond with availability and pricing information.

From a marketing standpoint, the information form is a tremendous asset. Experience has shown us that, in the photography industry, clients are much more likely to complete an information request form than to e-mail or call a photographer.

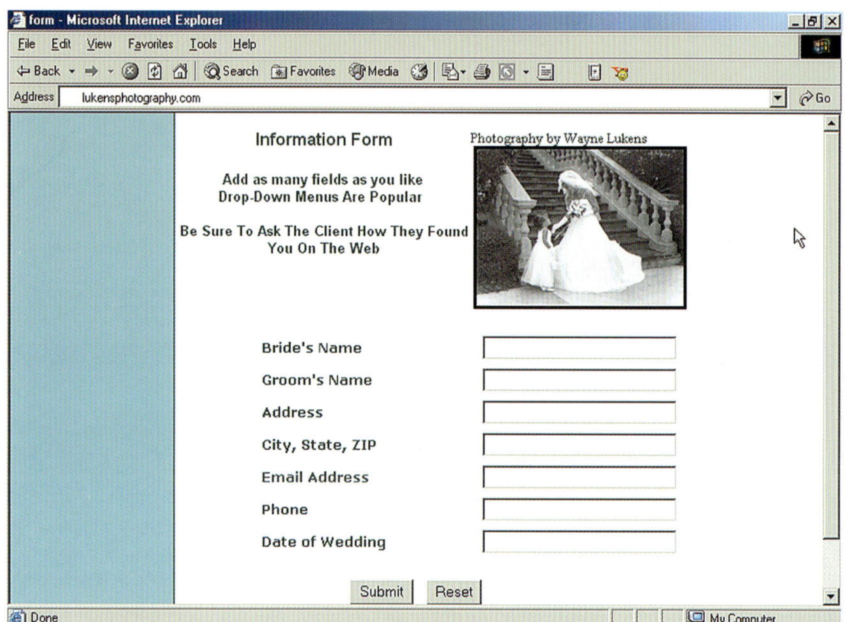

Figure 2-17: An Information Form puts you in touch with potential clients. Photograph by Wayne Lukens.

Creating the response/reply form is an easy process when using software like FrontPage. However, retrieving the information that is collected by your form is not so simple. Just putting a form on your web site does not mean it will work—in fact it will *not* work without proper setup behind the scenes. Some web-site hosting companies do not have the capability to process forms. Of those companies that do, each has a unique way of processing them. Before you contract with a hosting company it is very important that you ask if they can process response/reply forms. You want to be sure their capability includes sending form results via e-mail, otherwise your response/reply form will be of little or no use to either you or your visitors.

Photograph by Wayne Lukens.

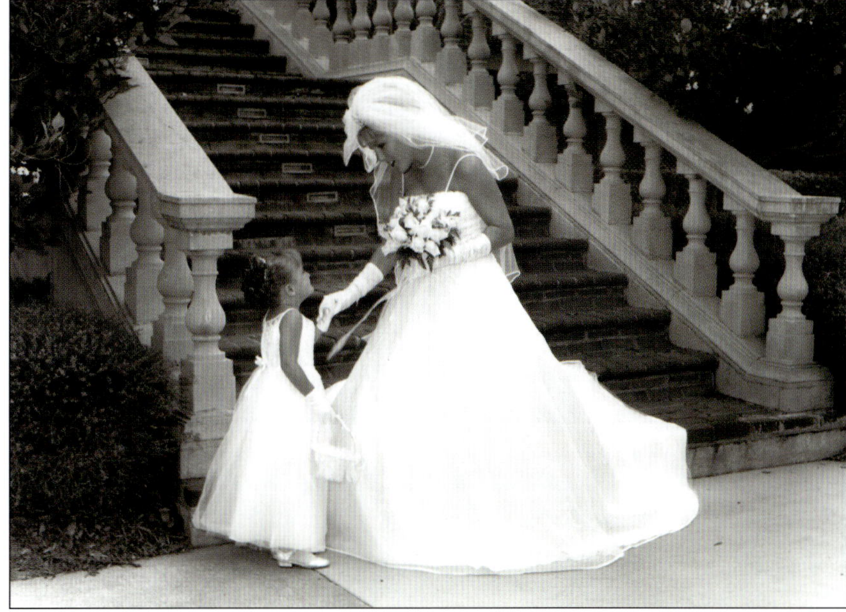

The information that the visitor provides in the form needs to be channeled through a CGI (Common Gateway Interface) program. The CGI program collects the data and processes it to e-mail messages, databases, or just saves it in text files. Your hosting company should provide these CGI programs at no extra cost. It is not always easy to implement a CGI program and you may need to hire a webmaster for a one-time setup session. Once your form is working properly there is no maintenance involved unless you want to make changes.

Links page—A web page containing hypertext links to related sites. For example, a wedding photographer's web page might include links to local florists, bakeries, bridal gown shops, receptions sites, etc.

Linking to Other Web Sites. A links page not only helps you to network with other vendors, it also provides for a higher ranking in some search-engine databases by demonstrating the popularity of your site. The Internet was created as an information tool. As such, you should offer more information than just your own services. For example, you can offer informational links on your site that lead to services that complement your own—perhaps a link to your film company of choice, or a link to a specific camera web site, etc. Always be sure to include "reciprocal links." Reciprocal linking is the art of getting other web sites to link to yours. Done properly, it's a powerful marketing tool that can improve your search-engine rankings and bring you highly qualified traffic.

If you can get enough web sites to link to yours it can help you greatly with what's known as "link popularity," which is one of the criteria used by most of the major search engines when ranking web sites. Theoretically, the more sites that are linked to yours, the better your popularity and the higher you rank.

► TEXT TO CAPTURE YOUR TARGET AUDIENCE

Be sure to match your good design with an appropriate choice of text. The rule of thumb here is *less is best!* Use phrases that will spark interest and keep the visitor on the site. State the services you provide in as few words as possible.

If the Internet is about information, why should you not include as much text as possible? Consider the fact that most visitors stay on your site for a total of thirty seconds on the first visit. This is certainly not long enough to read an entire monologue about how great you are. If too much information is offered, the client will have no reason to contact you. A little "mystery" is not a bad thing.

On the home page, the first page the viewer sees, it is especially important to use only essential text—let a few well-chosen words and images intrigue the viewer. For your home page, you might choose a phrase like, "Providing the finest in wedding, portrait and commercial photography. Photography since 1991." Using the word "free" is also a good way to entice clients—for example, you might mention your offer for a "Free On-Line Photography Consultation." If your company uses a slogan or advertising tagline, this should appear prominently on the front page.

Use only essential text—let a few well-chosen words and images intrigue the viewer.

Some slogans are so incredibly effective that they've become very widely recognized—"Don't leave home without it" (American Express), "The greatest show on earth" (Barnum and Bailey Circus), etc.. These sales slogans (or "ad tags") have generated millions of dollars in business because we can easily identify with each combination of words. Your ad tag is one of the most important elements for your site. The words should be professional and speak the truth about your personal expertise in your business.

Choose carefully considering all that you do and all that you have done. Some photographers hire professionals to create this unique addition to their site. Keep in mind that many slogans are copyrighted for private use only, so you can't just borrow a good one that you happen to like and should consider researching yours to make sure it's not already in use. As you work on developing an advertising slogan (tag line), consider the following questions:

- What is being advertised?
- To whom are you advertising?
- What do you know about your audience?
- What do you want them to do?

- What can you say that will get them to do that?
- What ideas might work?
- What is your key message?

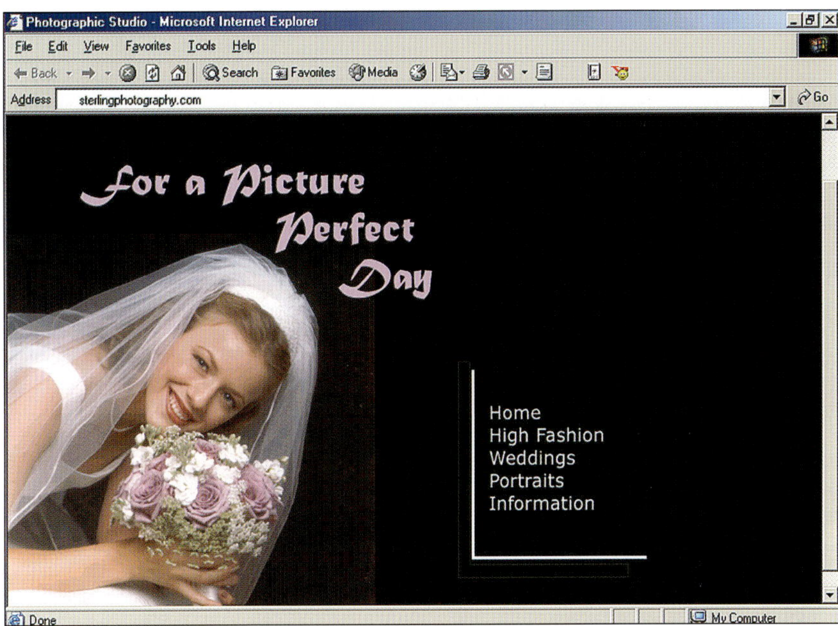

Figure 2-18: Web site showing an effective advertising slogan. Photography by J.R. Sterling.

In short, there are three easy steps to take to make sure visitors will feel motivated to complete the (response/reply) information form:

1. First capture the visitor's interest by having a pleasing front page (see Figure 2-18).
2. Generate interest with a "killer" ad tag.
3. Show them your finest images.

3. photoshop techniques

In this chapter you will learn Photoshop techniques that can be used to enhance your web site. Each example will demonstrate some of the capabilities of Photoshop. Once you recreate the example, you should then spend time experimenting with the other tools, colors, and effects. As you know from your photography experience, good results come from technical experience, artistic ability, and practice. Each sample is a stand-alone method, so you may choose the method which appeals to you.

It is assumed that you are already familiar with the tools and general use of Photoshop and image editing. If you need a beginner's course or just a refresher, you should refer to *Beginner's Guide to Adobe Photoshop* by Michelle Perkins, or *Traditional Photographic Effects with Adobe Photoshop* by Michelle Perkins and Paul Grant (both from Amherst Media).

THE BASICS

Computer monitors display images at 72dpi (pixels [or "dots"] per inch). Therefore, you should create and save your web-page images at this resolution. Using a resolution that is any higher won't improve the image quality and will take much longer to load—meaning visitors may get tired of waiting for images to appear and move on to another web site!

Backgrounds, buttons and most images may be saved as either GIF files or JPG files. The designer wants to keep the file size to a minimum, while balancing image quality versus file size. Whichever format gives the quality and smallest file size should be chosen.

GIF (Graphics Interchange Format)—A file format for digital images.

JPEG (Joint Photographic Expert Group)—A file format and method of data compression for digital images.

Your quality photography images, however, should be saved only as JPG format files, as they will retain more detail when viewed on the web. Photoshop offers a variety of file-size options for saving JPG files. Keep in mind that information is always lost in compression, however. Once compressed with JPG—even using the highest quality settings in Photoshop—the image will not be identical to the original. Compression ratios typically range from 10:1 to 100:1. The greater the compression the lower the quality and the smaller the file size. When you select a smaller file size, your images will load more quickly but will also be of a lower visual quality and may appear distorted. For this reason, you must decide on a compromise between quick download time (lower image quality) and higher quality (longer download time). We use low-quality-setting JPGs for the web, because they compress to small file sizes and look fine.

CREATING A GRADIENT BACKGROUND

Choosing the background for your web pages is an important decision, as it will determine the overall appearance of your page (see chapter 2). It also provides the backdrop for your images (much like a mat does for a print). You can add a contrasting color and interest to your page by placing a gradient color on the left edge of your pages. This section demonstrates the Photoshop steps to make a background with a gradient color and a vertical stripe along the left edge. As you practice making background pictures, keep in mind that they will be repeated on your page, stacked from top to bottom. Any vertical lines must be completely vertical. A non-vertical or slanted line will result in a zig-zag line down your web page, instead of a straight one.

Figure 3-1

While most monitors display an image that is 800 pixels wide, some visitor may use a larger monitor screen or screen settings greater than 800 pixels wide. Therefore, it is good practice to make your background images 1024 pixels wide.

Step 1—In Photoshop, go to the File menu and choose New to make a new file. Set the width of the file to 1024 pixels and the height to 50 pixels. Set the resolution to 72 pixels/inch and set the Mode to RGB color.

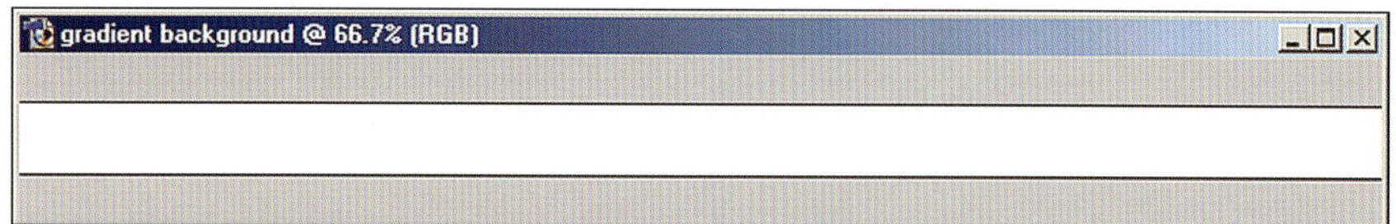

Figure 3-2

Step 2—Decide on your main background color (this example uses black). Click on the foreground color swatch in the Toolbox and create the desired color using the Color Picker, or mix a color using the Color palette (if this is not visible, go to Window>Color). Select the Paint Bucket tool and click anywhere in the new image fill the picture area with the color you selected.

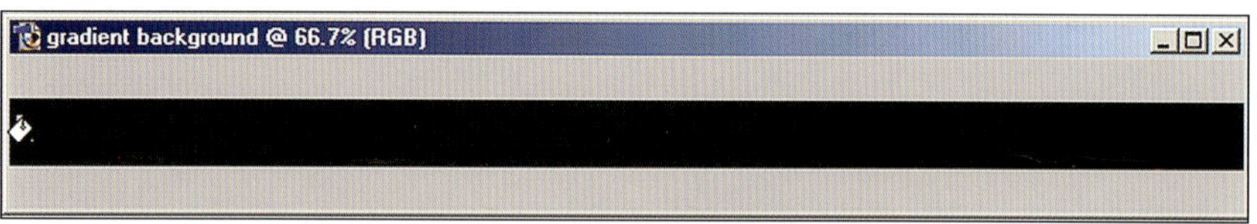

Figure 3-3

Step 3—Decide on a color for the gradient, this example uses forest green. Reverse the Foreground Color Swatch with the Background Color Swatch to move black to the background color. Click on the foreground color swatch in the Toolbox and choose your color using the Color Picker or mix a color using the color palette.

Step 4—Select the Rectangular Marquee tool. In the Options bar at the top pf the screen, set the feather option to 0 pixels. Click and drag a rectangle across the left end of the picture from top to bottom. This will define your gradient area. This is actually optional, but helps you visualize where your gradient will end.

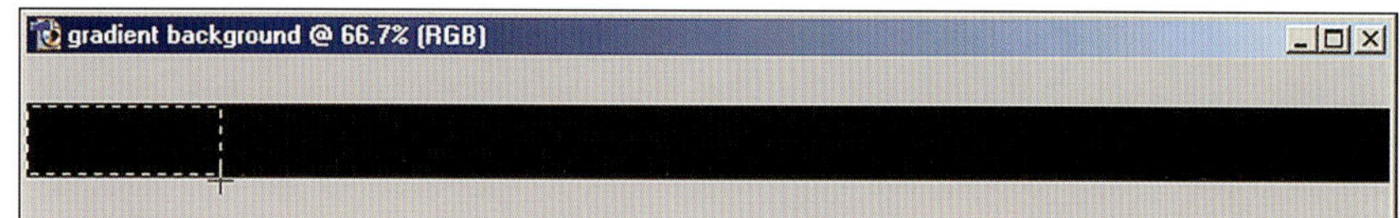

Figure 3-4

Step 5—Select the Gradient tool. The gradient tool has several options; select the horizontal option shown in Figure 3-5a. Move your cursor over the far left edge of the picture, press and hold the Shift key, then click and drag to the right edge of the selected gradient area. Release the mouse button. Your gradient color will appear at the left edge and blends into the background color as you move to the right.

Figure 3-5a

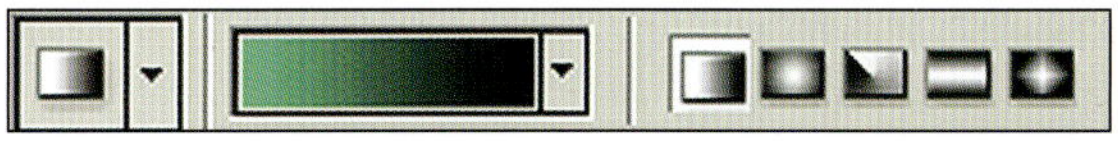

Figure 3-5b

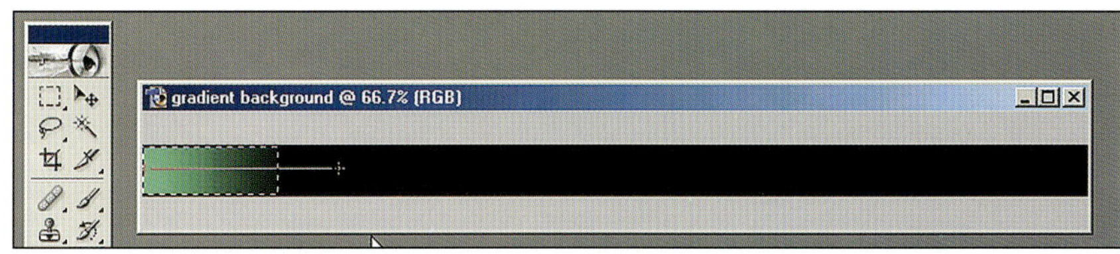

Step 6—To deselect the rectangular gradient area, choose Select>Deselect.

Step 7—Next, you need to select a color for the vertical line. This examples uses pale green. To select the color you want, click on the foreground color swatch in the toolbox and create a color using the Color Picker, or mix a color using the Color palette.

Step 8—Select the Line tool. In the options bar, set the line's Weight to 3 pixels. At the left and of the image (above the gradient area) click and hold the left mouse button. Draw a line vertically to below the colored area, then release the mouse button (holding the Shift key while you draw your line will ensure that it is perfectly vertical). By starting above and finishing below the borders you will ensure a continuous line from top to bottom. When your image is repeated in your web page you will see a continuous line with no breaks where the repeating images connect.

Step 9—Save the file in the JPG or GIF format. There is no need to save this picture with high quality (large file size) since there is very little detail. Keep all of your file sizes to the minimum needed to produce a quality look; remember large file sizes take longer to load into your viewer's browser.

Figure 3-6

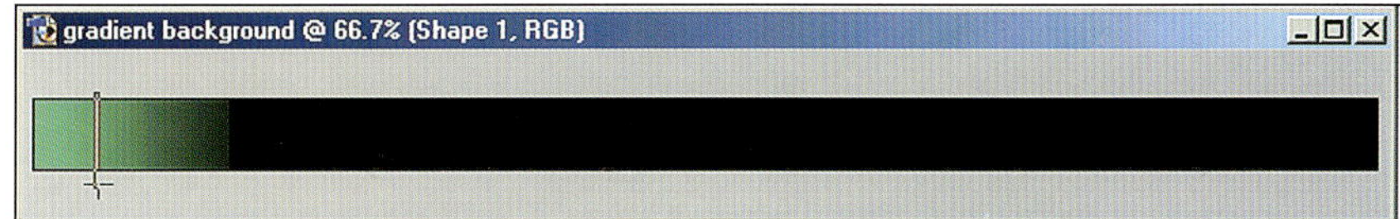

This picture strip can now be used as a web page background. The picture simply repeats on your web page from top to bottom. You can see the completed page in Chapter 2. Figures 3-7 and 3-8 are some other examples of gradient backgrounds:

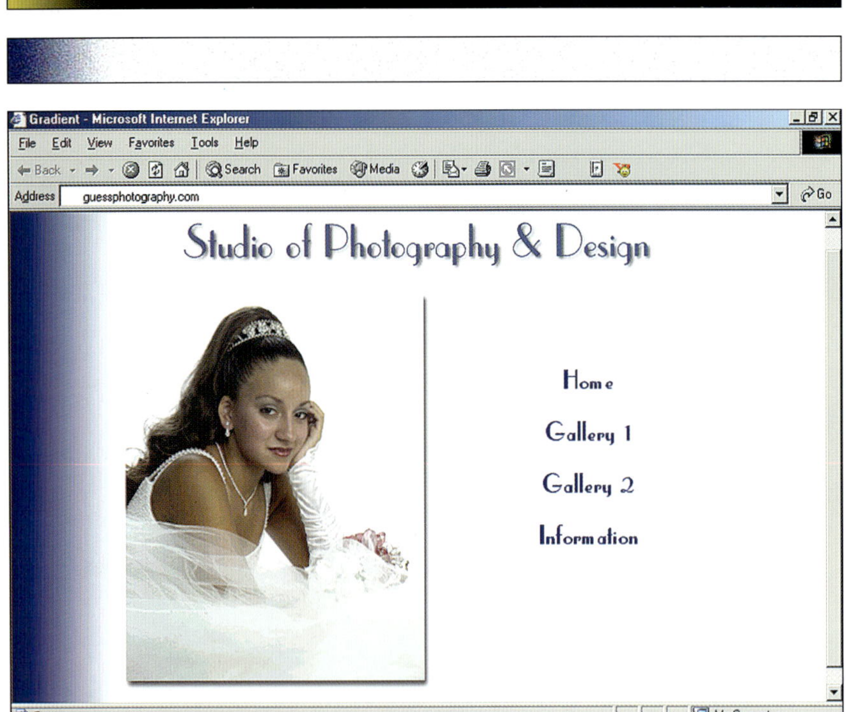

Figure 3-7a: Sample gradient.

Figure 3-7b: Sample gradient.

Figure 3-8: Web page using the blue and white gradient background featured above. Photography by Guillermo Rodriguez.

CREATING A TEXTURED BACKGROUND

Photoshop has several filters that can be used to create interesting textured backgrounds. Figure 3-9 simply shows the addition of noise (Filter>Noise>Add Noise) to a selected color, however you should try several of the filter options to determine the look you want.

Filters—Built-in functions of Photoshop that the user can apply to enhance their images. There are four basic filter types. Filters that improve image quality, filters that add artistic effects, filters that add special effects and filters that perform technical corrections.

Figure 3-9

The textured background picture will repeat itself on the web page starting at the top left corner and progress to the right and downward until the page is filled. Using a size of 128 pixels x 128 pixels will ensure that the patterns blend seamlessly when they lay side by side. If you are going to use multiple background images in contrasting colors on your web pages (which is recommended), you should create a textured background for each color. You will see the effect of using these contrasting backgrounds in the example that follows these instructions.

Step 1—From the File menu choose New to make a new file (Figure 3-10). Set the Image Size to 128 pixels wide and 128 pixels high. Set the Resolution to 72 pixels/inch and the Mode to RGB color.

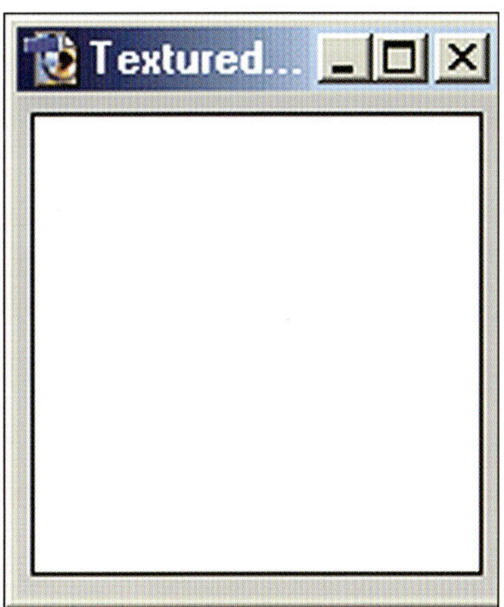

Figure 3-10

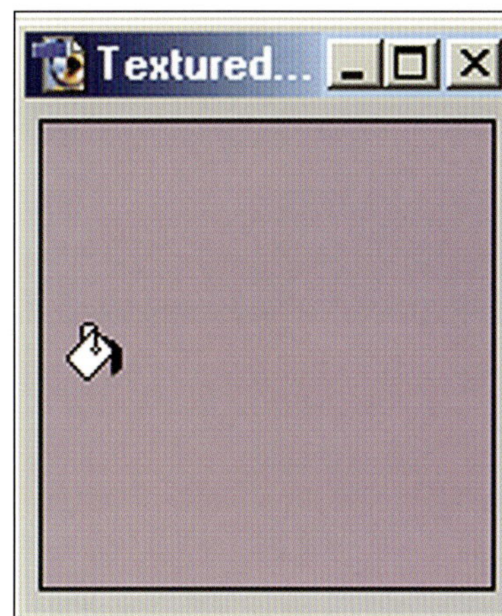

Figure 3-11

Step 2—Click on the foreground color swatch in the Toolbox and create a color using the Color Picker, or mix a color using the Color palette. Select the Paint Bucket tool and click withing the picture area to fill it with the foreground color (Figure 3-11).

Noise—An effect that allows you to add the digital equivalent of film grain to images.

Step 3—From the Filter menu choose Noise and then choose Add Noise to display the Add Noise dialog box. Set the Amount to 3 and click the Gaussian radio button. Next, check the Monochromatic box and click OK.

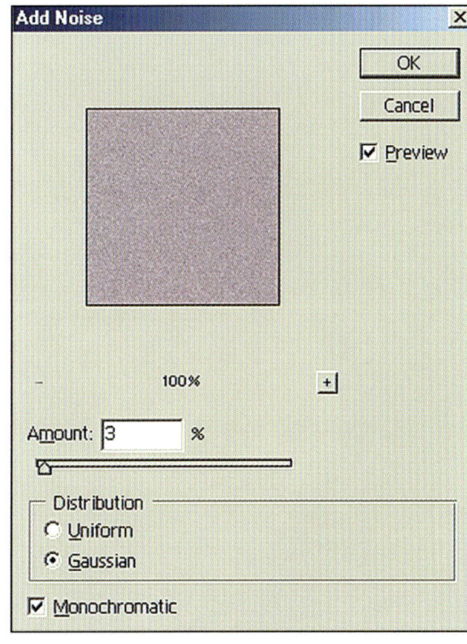

Figure 3-12

Figure 3-13

Step 4—Save this image as a JPG format file or a GIF format file.

In the sample page (Figure 3-14) there are three background colors used for effect. Each color was processed through Photoshop to create the texture. Textured backgrounds soften the look of the page. They also give a three dimensional feel to the page without detracting from or overpowering the photographs.

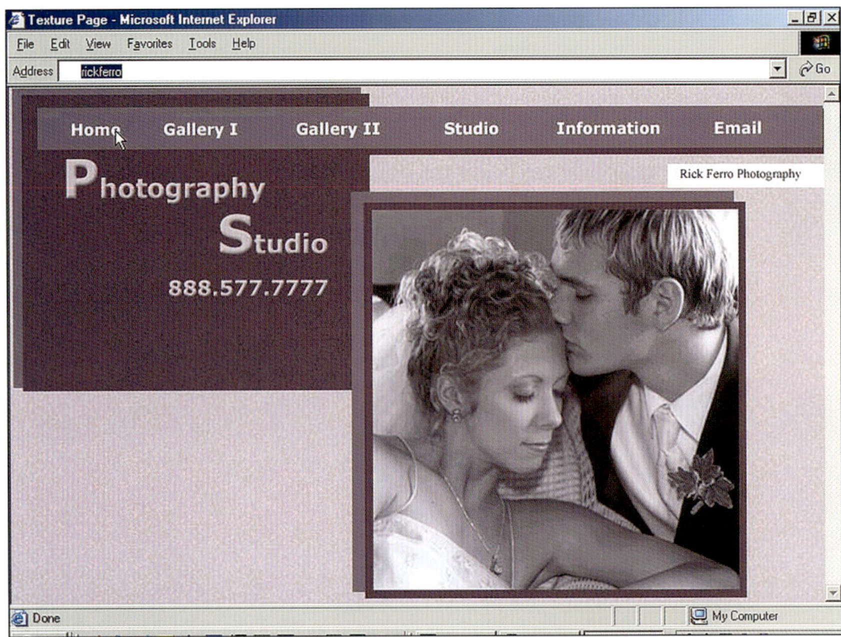

Figure 3-14: A web page created with three textured background images. The background images are used as page background, table background, and layer background.

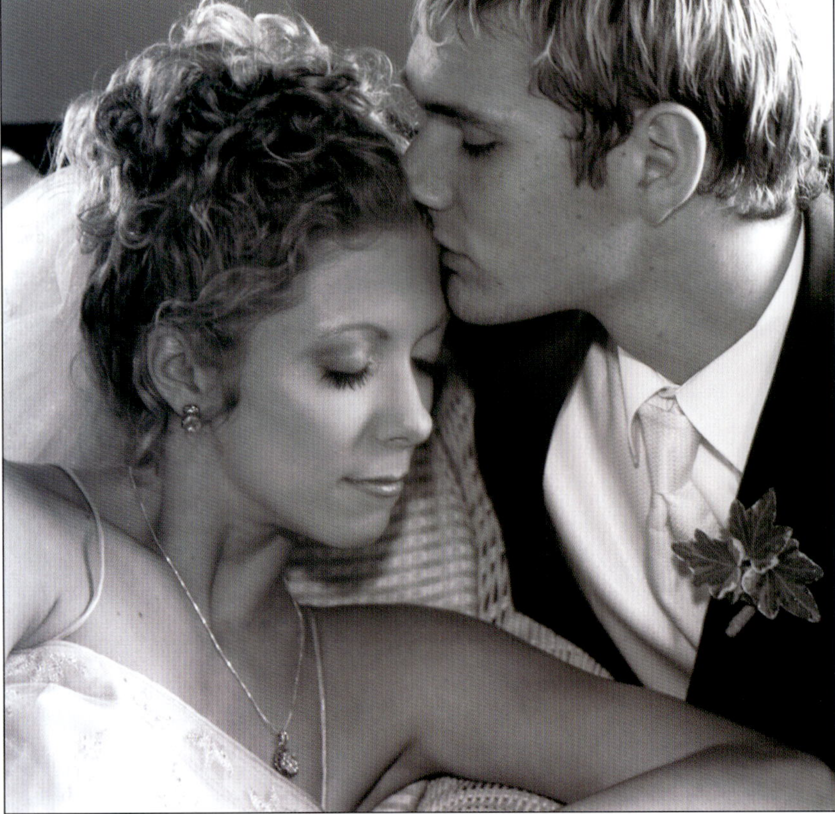

Photograph by Rick Ferro.

► CREATING THE ROUND BUTTON

In web design, a button invites the user to click on it to move on to new information. You can select the size, color and shape of your button based on your personal tastes and needs (Figure 3-15).

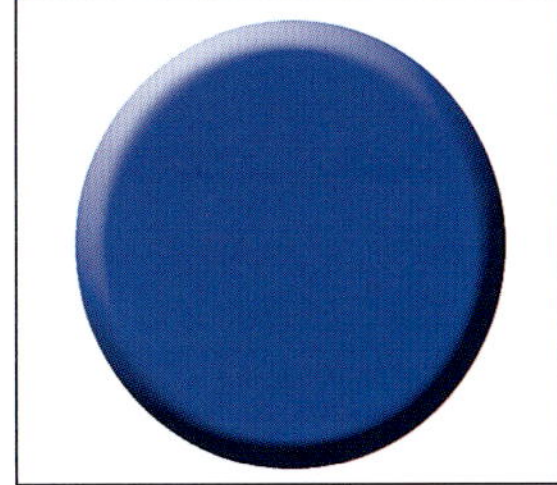

Figure 3-15

Step 1—From the File menu choose New. Set the size of the new image file to 40 pixels wide and 40 pixels high. Set the color mode to RGB. If you plan to save the button as a GIF file, set the Contents of the image to Transparent. If you plan to save your button as a JPG, set the background color in the Toolbox to the same color as you are using in your web page background. Then, in the New window, set the Contents of the new image file to Background Color (Figure 3-16).

Step 2—From the Layer menu choose New and then choose Layer.

Step 3—Select the Elliptical Marquee tool. Click and drag a circle that runs from edge to edge across the project window (Figure 3-17).

Step 4—Click on the foreground color swatch in the Toolbox to activate the Color Picker. Select a color for the button and click OK.

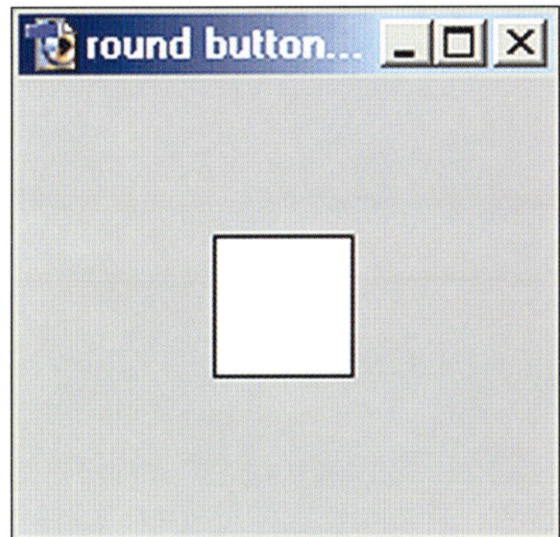

Figure 3-16

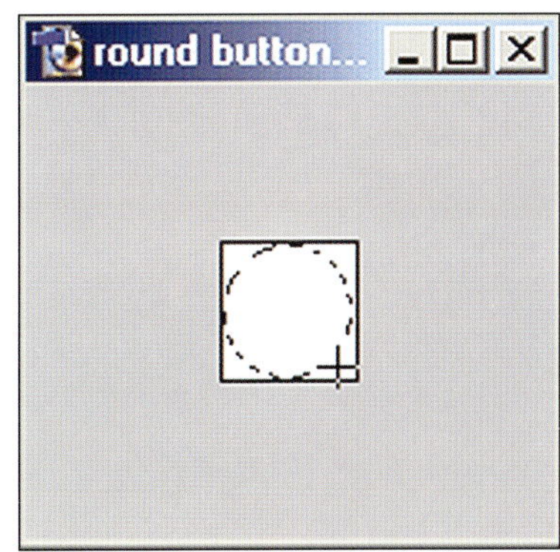

Figure 3-17

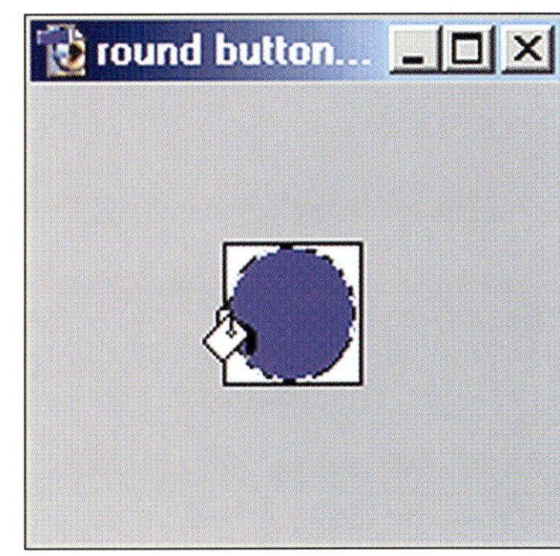

Figure 3-18

Step 5—Select the Paint Bucket tool and click within the selection to paint the circle (Figure 3-18).

Step 6—Next, you need to bevel the circle edges. From the Layer menu choose Layer Style then choose Bevel and Emboss. In the pop-up window, adjust the options to your liking then click OK.

Step 7—From the Select menu choose Deselect. Save the button as a JPG or GIF file type (see Step 1). You may wish to flatten the image (Layer>Flatten Image) to reduce file size.

CREATING THE RECTANGULAR BUTTON

Step 1—From the File menu choose New. Set the size of the new image to 125 pixels wide and 24 pixels high. Set the color mode to RGB. The background can be set to any color—it won't show in the final image (Figure 3-19).

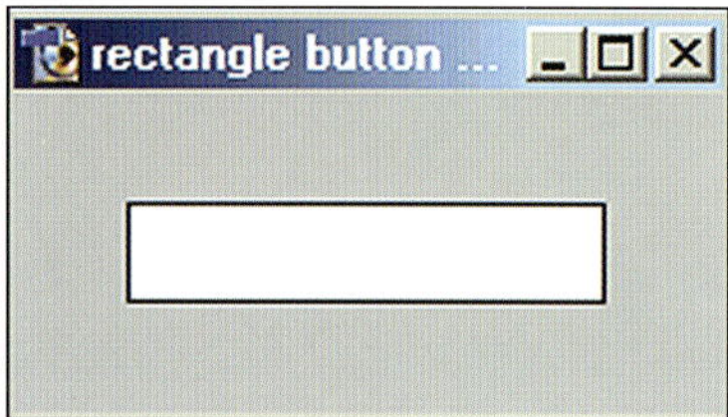

Figure 3-19

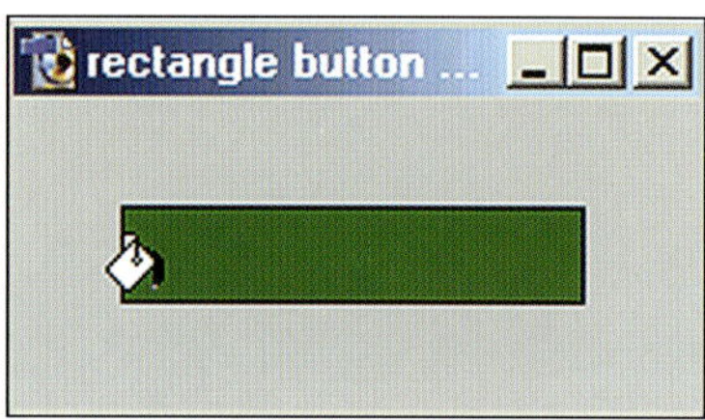

Figure 3-20

Step 2—From the Layer menu, choose New and then choose Layer.

Step 3—Click on the foreground color swatch in the Toolbox to select a color for the button. Pick a color from the Color Picker and click OK.

Step 4—Select the Paint Bucket tool. Place the Paint Bucket tool over the image and click (Figure 3-20).

Step 5—From the Layer menu choose Layer Style then choose Bevel and Emboss. In the dialog box, adjust the options to your liking then click OK (Figure 3-21).

Step 6—From the Filter menu select Noise then choose Add Noise. From the Add Noise dialog box set the Amount to 3, click the

Gaussian radio button, and check the Monochromatic check box (Figure 3-22). Then click OK (Figure 3-23).

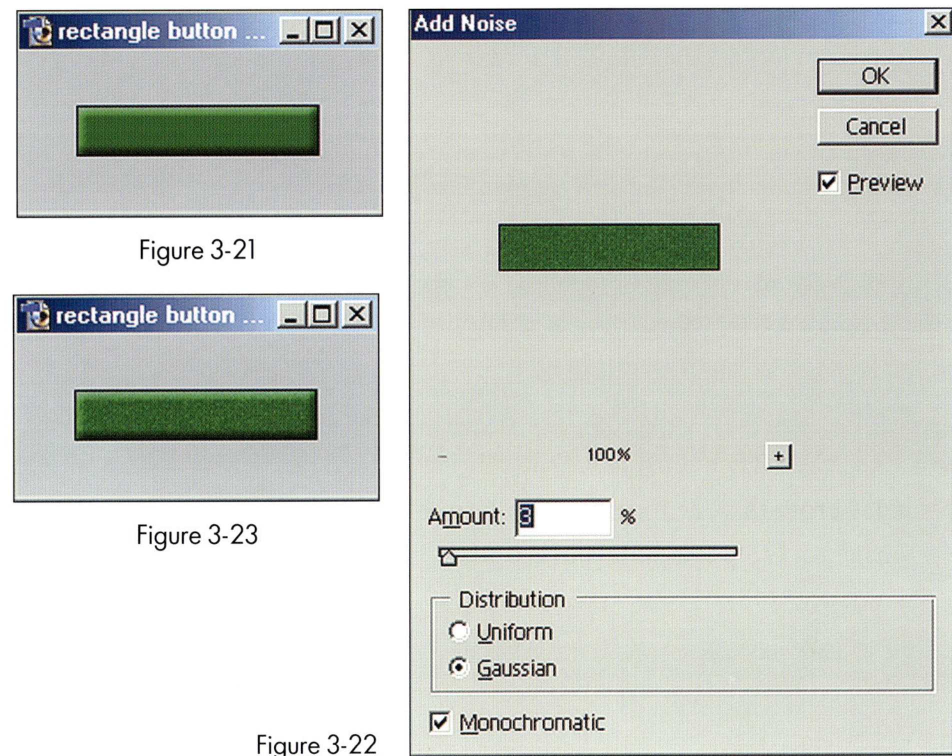

Figure 3-21

Figure 3-23

Figure 3-22

Step 7—Select the Type tool from the Toolbox. Choose a font, type size, and font color from the Options bar at the top of the screen (Figure 3-24).

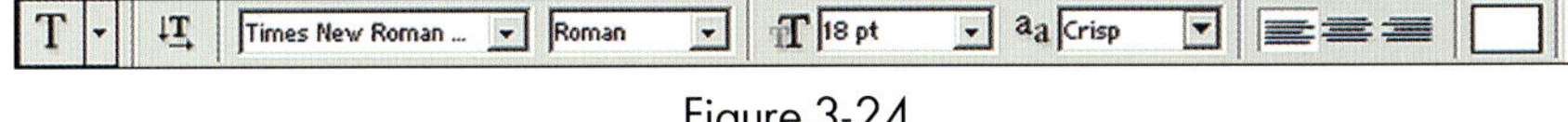

Figure 3-24

Step 8—Place the cursor at the left side of the image and click. Type the title for the button. Select the Move tool from the Toolbox and use the pointer to center the text in the image.

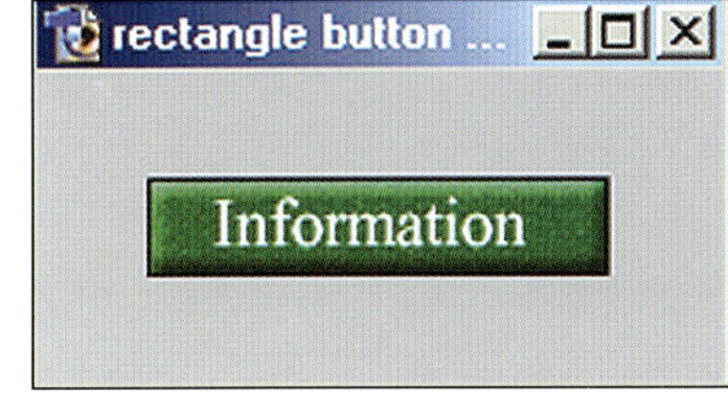

Figure 3-25

Step 9—Save the image as a JPG or GIF file type. You may wish to flatten the image (Layer>Flatten Image) to reduce file size.

Step 10—If you are making several buttons of the same style with different titles, it is easy to make them all at this time. Select the

Type tool from the Toolbox. Point at the beginning of the text, then click and and drag across the word or words. Release the mouse button and the text is now highlighted. Type the title for the new button, then go to File>Save As and save the file with a new file name.

► CREATING THE CYLINDRICAL BUTTON

Step 1—From the File menu choose New. Set the size of the new image file to 125 pixels wide and 24 pixels high. Set the color mode to RGB (Figure 3-26).

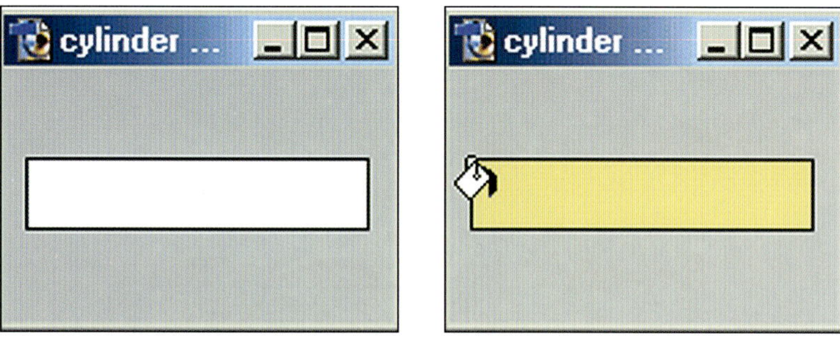

Figure 3-26　　Figure 3-27

Step 2—Click on the foreground color swatch in the Toolbox to activate the Color Picker. Then, create a color using the following RGB values: R=247/G=220/B=125. Click on the background color swatch in the Toolbox and create a color using the following RGB amounts: R=117/G=118/B=42. Select the Paint Bucket tool and click within the image area to fill it with the foreground color (Figure 3-27).

Step 3—Select the Gradient tool from the Toolbox. Select the Vertical Gradient from the Options bar at the top of the screen.

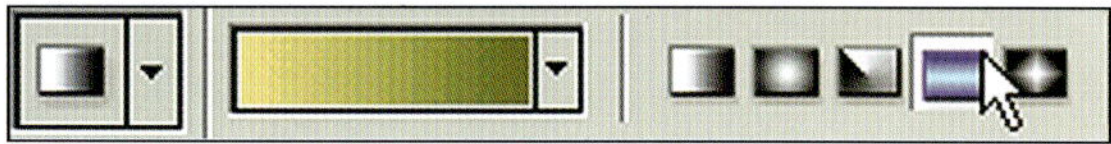

Figure 3-28

Step 4—Point at the center of the image, press and hold the Shift key, then click and drag the cursor straight down to the bottom of the image (Figure 3-29) and release the mouse button (Figure 3-30).

Step 5—Select the Type tool. Choose a font, type size and color from the Options bar at the top of the screen (Figure 3-31).

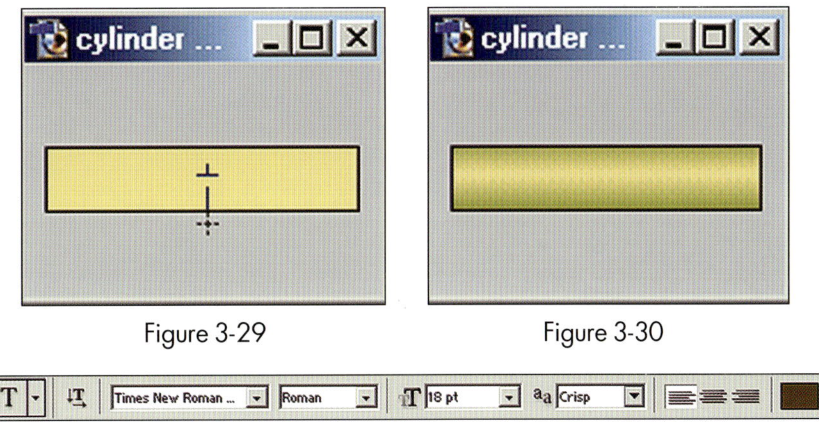

Figure 3-29

Figure 3-30

Figure 3-31

Step 6—Place the cursor at the left side of the image and click. Type the title of the button. Select the Move tool from the Toolbox and use the pointer to center the text in the button.

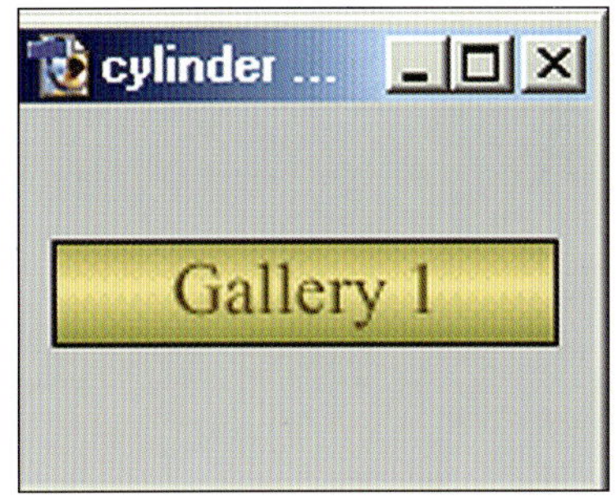

Figure 3-32

Step 7—Save the image as a JPG or GIF file type. You may wish to flatten the image (Layer>Flatten Image) to reduce file size.

Step 8—If you are making several buttons of the same style with different titles, it is easy to make them all at this time. Select the Type tool from the Toolbox. Point at the beginning of the text, then click and drag across the word or words. Release the mouse button and the text is now highlighted. Type the title for the new button, center the text as in Step 6, then go to File>Save As and save the file with a new file name.

CREATING A TEXT LOGO

Photoshop offers many text-style features, including embossing and shadowing. You should also check out the Actions palette for some interesting text effects like confetti, waves, water reflection, wood grain and brushed metal. This session demonstrates how you can use your company name and a simple Photoshop filter to make a logo. When you are beginning this project, open a window that is plenty

Actions—A set of steps that are saved as a single unit. This set can then be applied to enact that precise series of steps to single or multiple images.

large so that you can toss in a lot of ideas. Then you can begin to narrow them down to the final layout, and finally crop and size the image to the desired shape.

In this example, the logo will be used on a web page that has a black background, so we will start with a black background in the Photoshop work area.

Step 1—From the File menu choose New to make a new file. Set the size of the image to 400 pixels wide and 300 pixels high. Set the resolution to 72 pixels/inch and the Mode to RGB color. Set the background color to white.

Step 2—Click on the foreground color swatch in the Toolbox and set the color to black. Select the Paint Bucket tool click within the image area to fill it with the color.

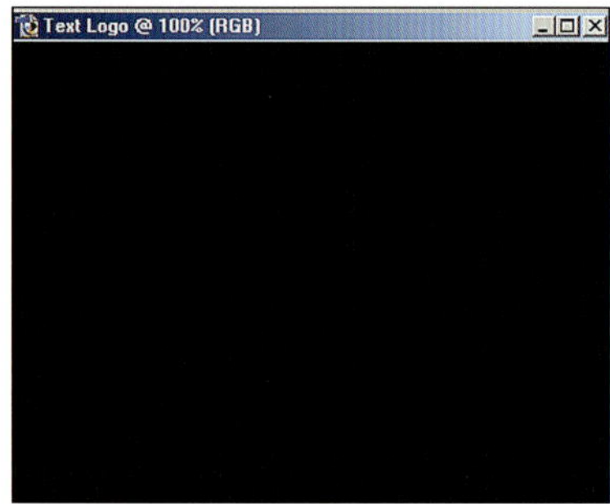

Figure 3-33

Step 3—From the Filter menu choose Render and then click on Lens Flare. In the Lens Flare dialog box choose the 50–300mm zoom button (Figure 3-34). Point and click at different loca-

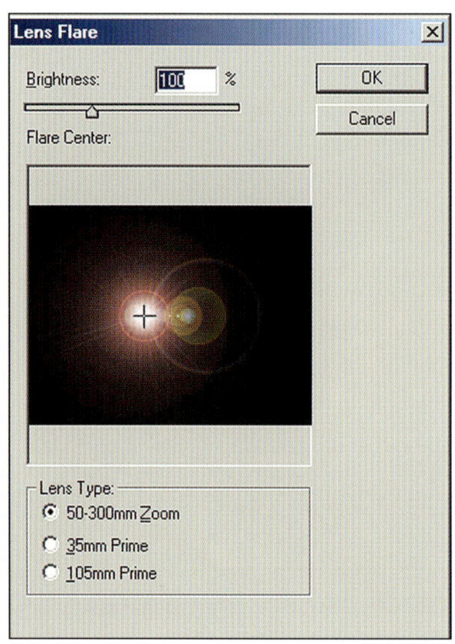

Figure 3-34

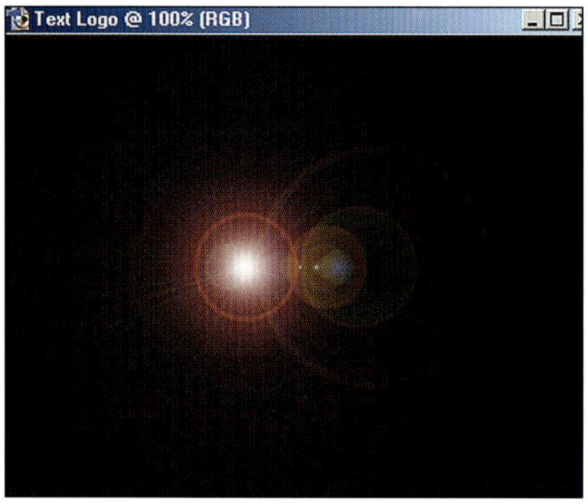

Figure 3-35

tions in the black box and experiment with the different effects. In this example, the area chosen was slightly to the left of center (Figure 3-35). Set the Brightness to 100% and click OK.

Step 4—Select the Type tool from the Toolbox. Click anywhere inside the workspace window. Select a font, font size, and font color. In this example, the first letter of the first word ("P") was set to a size of 60 points and the color was set to grey. We then changed the font size to 36 and typed the remainder of the word "Photography." When your text is complete, select the Move tool from the Toolbox and position the word as you like.

Step 5—Repeat step 4 for the remainder of words in your company name.

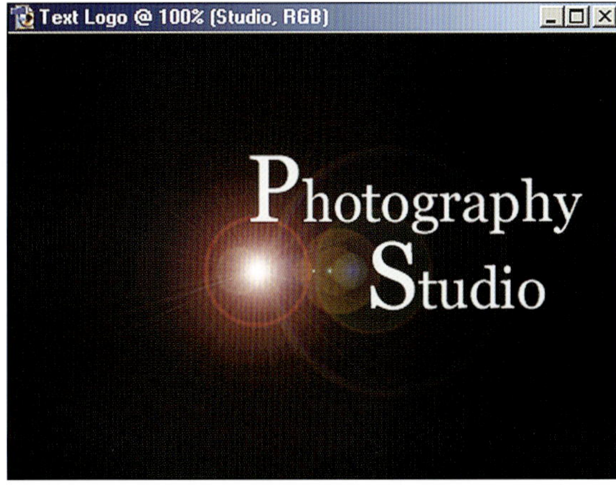

Figure 3-36

Step 6—If you like, you can now add any text effects you want. For the effect seen in this example, go to the Layer menu, choose Layer Style and then click on Bevel and Emboss. In the dialog box that appears, choose the parameters that provide the text effect you want, then click OK.

Step 7—To apply the same effect to the other text layers click on the Layer that has been edited (Figure 3-37). Then go to

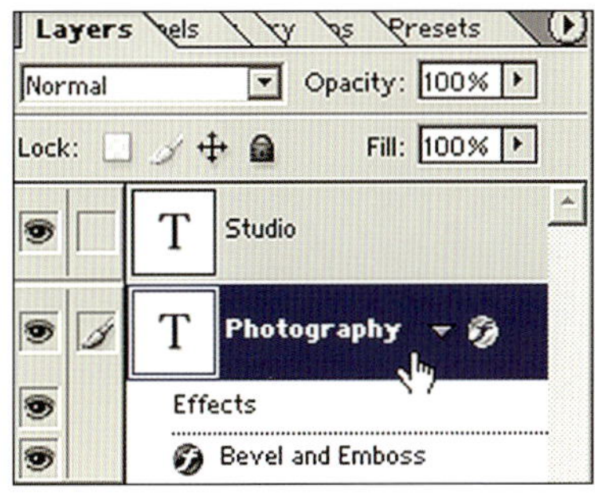

Figure 3-37

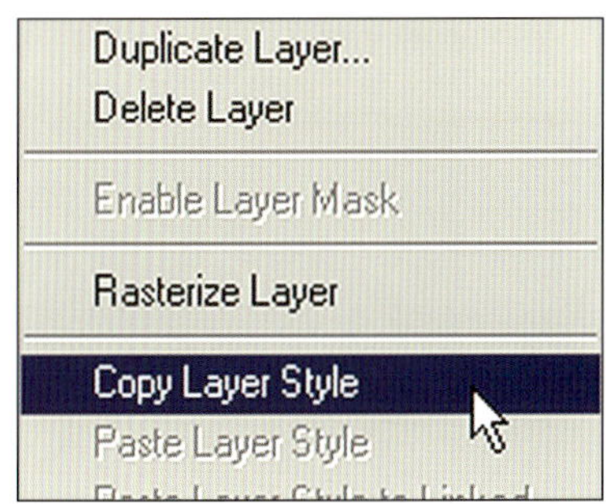

Figure 3-38

Layer>Layer Style>Copy Layer Style (Figure 3-38). Click on a new text layer (one to which you want to apply the style [Figure 3-39]) and go to Layer>Layer Style>Paste Layer Style (Figure 3-40). You will see the text in the window change to display the same Bevel and Emboss effects as the original.

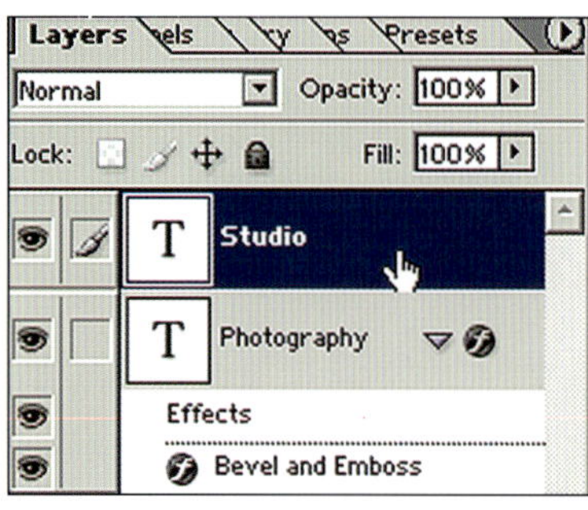

Figure 3-39

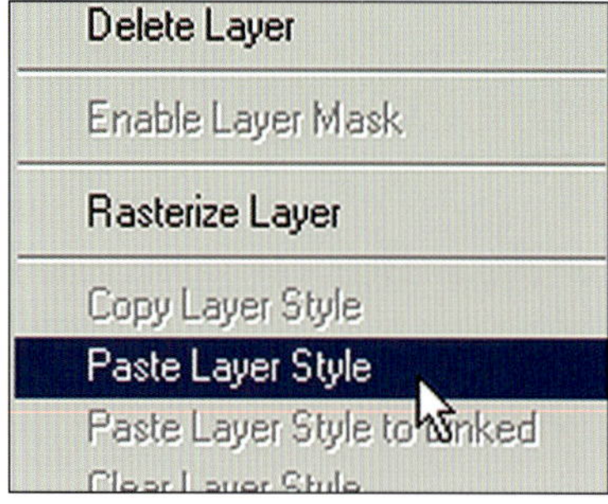

Figure 3-40

Step 8—Select the Crop tool from the Toolbox. Click and drag over the desired area and hit Enter (or double click within the crop area) to crop to the final size.

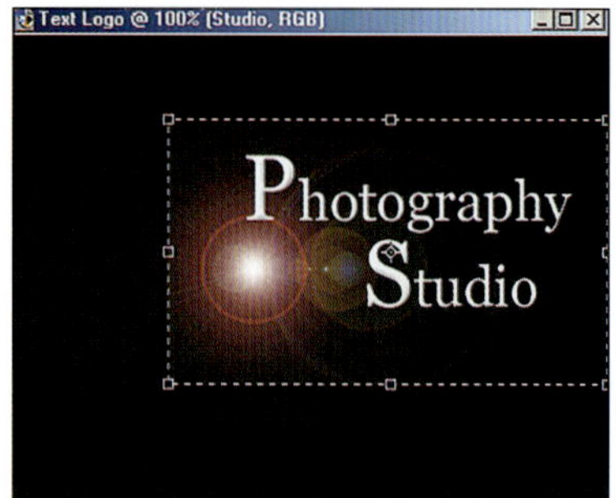

Figure 3-41

Step 9—You can now resize the logo to fit in your web page. From the Image menu choose Image Size. Size your image to your desired dimensions. Save the logo as a JPG format file with a medium quality setting. You may wish to flatten the image (Layer>Flatten Image) to reduce file size.

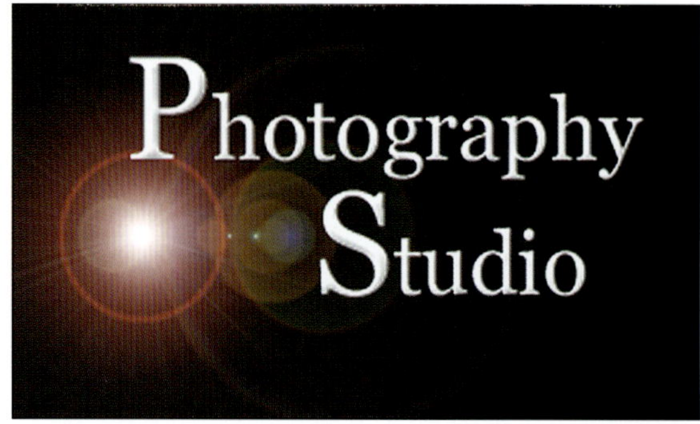

Figure 3-42

► CREATING A LOGO USING AN IMAGE

Using one of your favorite images in your logo design and displaying your company name prominently is an artful way to introduce yourself to prospective clients. It also takes advantage of the usable space on your web page. The photograph used in this example has previously been edited using methods not covered in this book. If you'd like to learn how to accomplish this handcolored effect, please refer to *Traditional Photographic Effects with Adobe Photoshop* (Amherst Media) by Michelle Perkins and Paul Grant or *Wedding Photography with Adobe Photoshop* (Amherst Media) by Rick Ferro and Deborah Lynn Ferro.

Step 1—From the File menu choose Open. In the selection window locate the file of the image you are going to use for your logo. Click on the file name to select it, then click the Open button.

Figure 3-43

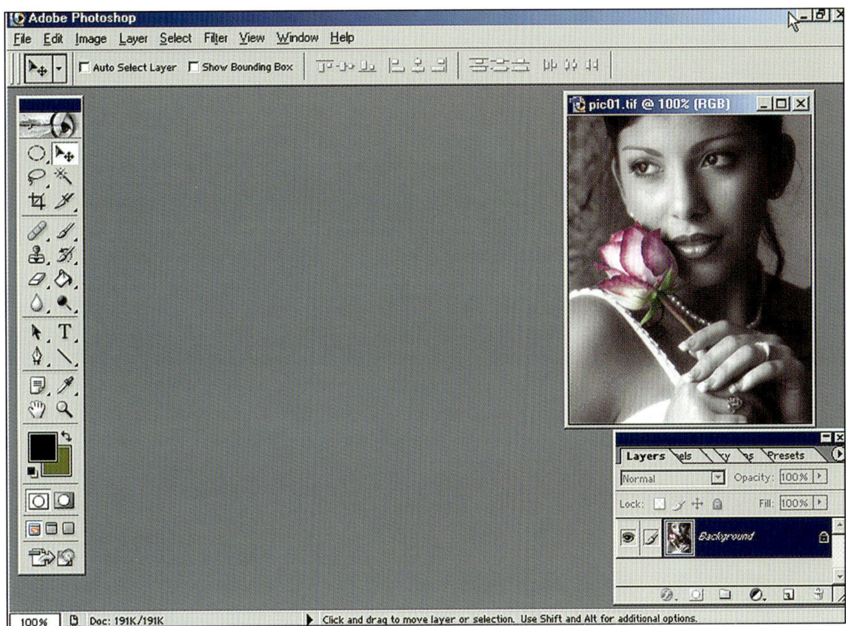

Step 2—From the Image menu choose Image Size. In the Image Size dialog box, go to the Pixel Dimensions settings. For portrait-style (vertical) pictures, enter 300 pixels in the *Height* box and click OK. For landscape-style (horizontal) pictures, type 300 pixels in the *Width* box and click OK (Figure 3-44).

Step 3—From the File menu choose New. In the dialog box, type 400 pixels in the Width window and 400 in the Height window. Set the resolution to 72 and the Mode to RGB Color

(Figure 3-45). Click OK. You now have two working windows open (Figure 3-46).

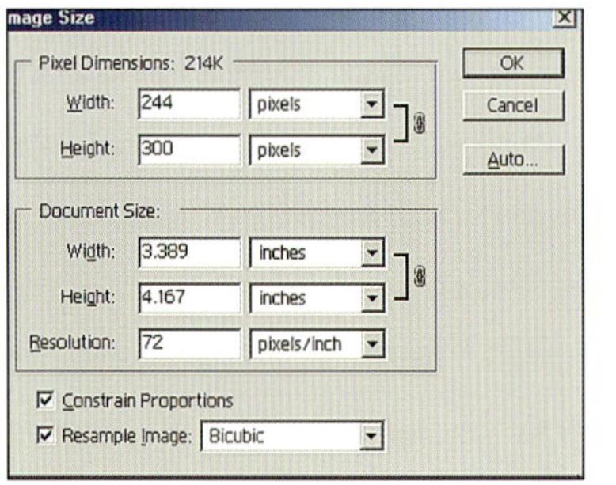

Figure 3-44

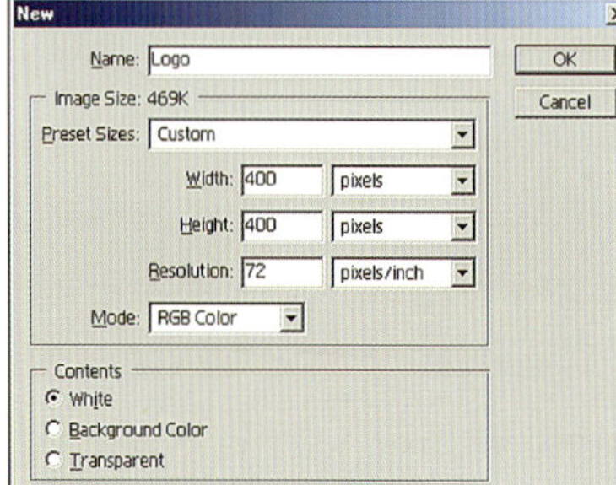

Figure 3-45

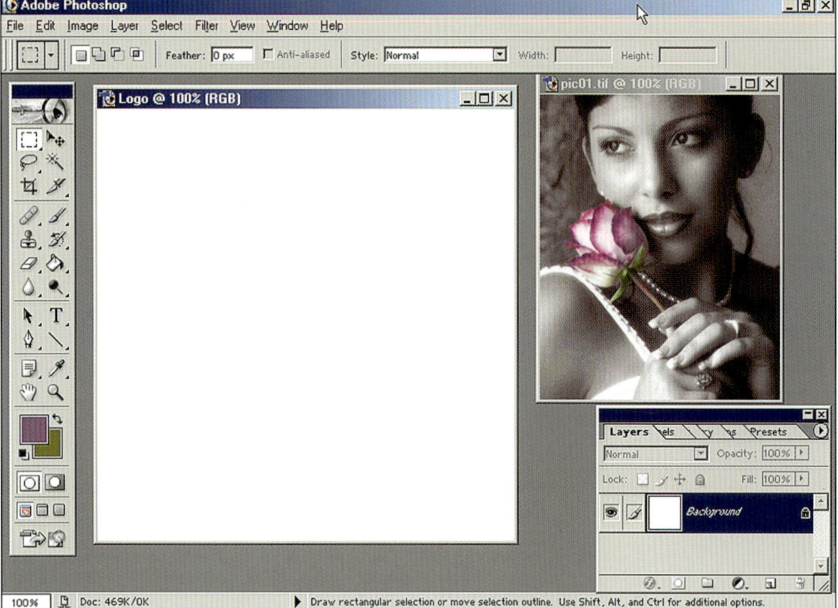

Figure 3-46

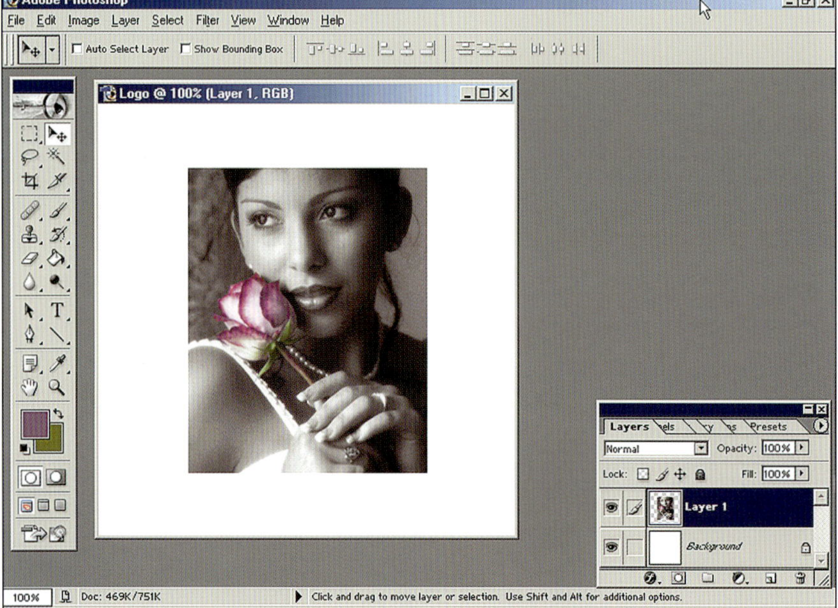

Figure 3-47

Step 4—Select the Move tool from the Toolbox. Point and click on the photograph once to make it the active window. Move your cursor over the photograph, then click and drag the picture into the larger empty window. Release the mouse button and a copy of the photograph is now in the new window. Use the Move tool to center the photograph in the larger image area (Figure 3-47). Close the photograph image file.

Step 5—In the Layers palette, change the Opacity to 55% for Layer 1. You can either enter this value inside the Opacity window or click and drag the slider bar.

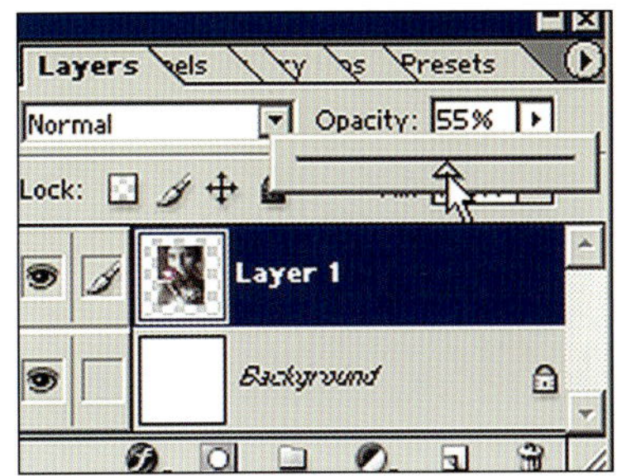

Figure 3-48

Step 6—In the Layers palette, click on the Background Layer to activate it. From the Layer menu, choose New, and then choose Layer. In the Layer dialog box you can name the layer or use the default name, then click OK. Next, you need to choose a color for the background rectangle (shown in lavender in Figure 3-54). To do this, click on the foreground color swatch in the Toolbox. In the Color Picker, select a color that will blend with the colors of your photograph, then click OK. For this example the color is R=136/G=95/B=129.

Step 7—Select the Rectangular Marquee tool from the Toolbox. Be sure that Feather is set to 0 in the options bar at the top of the screen.

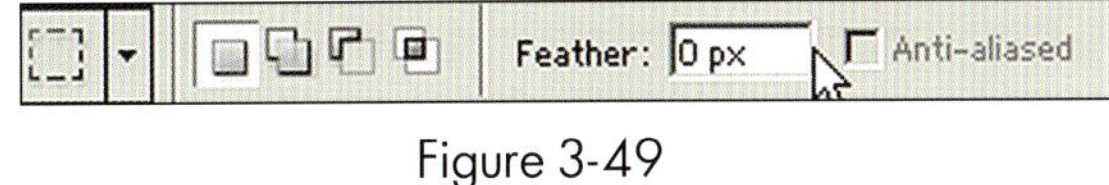

Figure 3-49

Press and hold the Control key and click on Layer 1 to select the entire picture. Then, activate the new layer in the Layers palette (Figure 3-50).

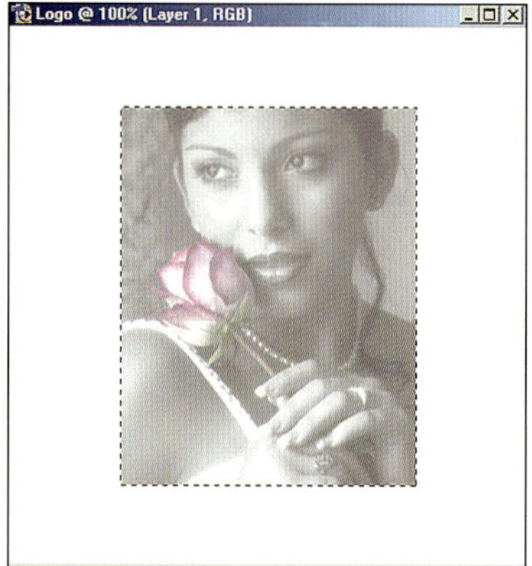

Figure 3-50

Step 8—From the Edit menu choose Fill. In the Fill dialog box, choose Foreground Color and click OK. Select the Move tool from the Toolbox, then click and hold inside the now-colored rectangle to move it up and to the right. In the Layers information box change the Opacity to 57% for Layer 2. From the Select menu choose Deselect.

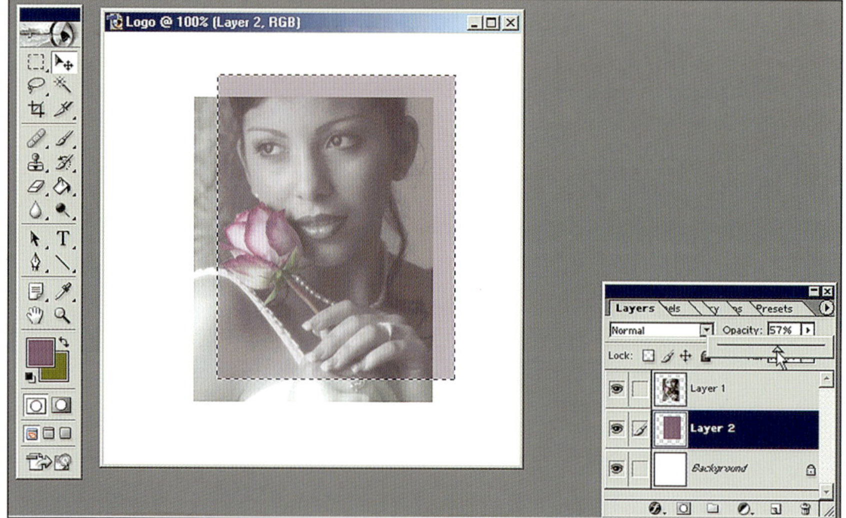

Figure 3-51

Step 9—Select the Type tool from the Toolbox. Click anywhere inside the workspace window. Select a font, font size, and font color (Figure 3-52). In this example, the first letter of the first word ("P") was set to a font size of 72 points, and the color was set to R=68/G=30/B=31. When you are done typing, select the Move tool from the Toolbox and position the letter (or word) as you like.

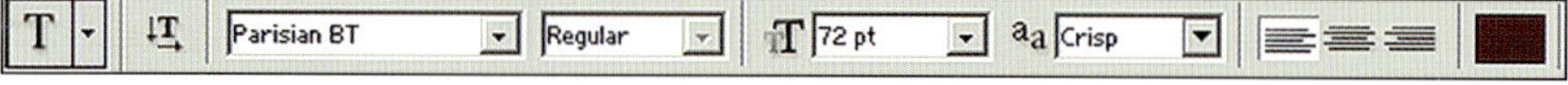

Figure 3-52

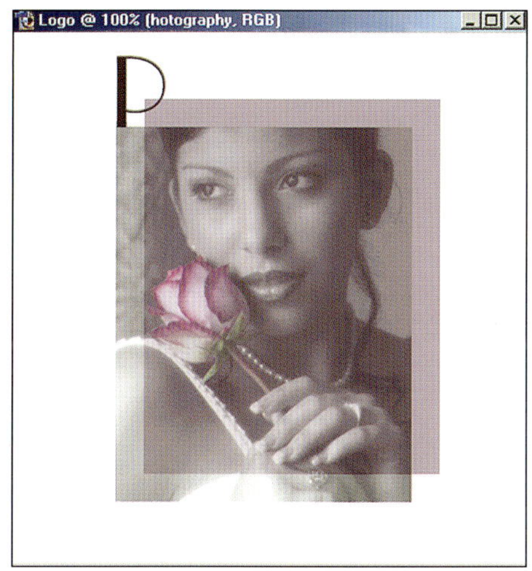

Figure 3-53

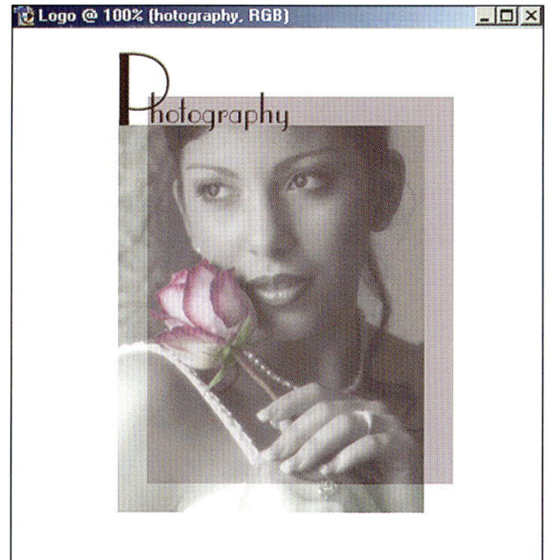

Figure 3-54

Step 10—Select the Type tool from the Toolbox. Click anywhere inside the workspace window. Select a font, font size, and font color. Here, we completed the word "Photography" using a font size of 30 points and in a dark color that complemented the photo and background rectangle (R=68/G=30/B=31). When you are done typing, select the Move tool from the Toolbox and position the letter (or word) as you like. Repeat Steps 9 and 10 for the rest of the words in your company name and/or logo (Figure 3-54).

Step 11—Select the Crop tool from the Toolbox. Crop your logo to its final size. Save your image as a JPG file. You may wish to flatten the image (Layer>Flatten Image) to reduce file size.

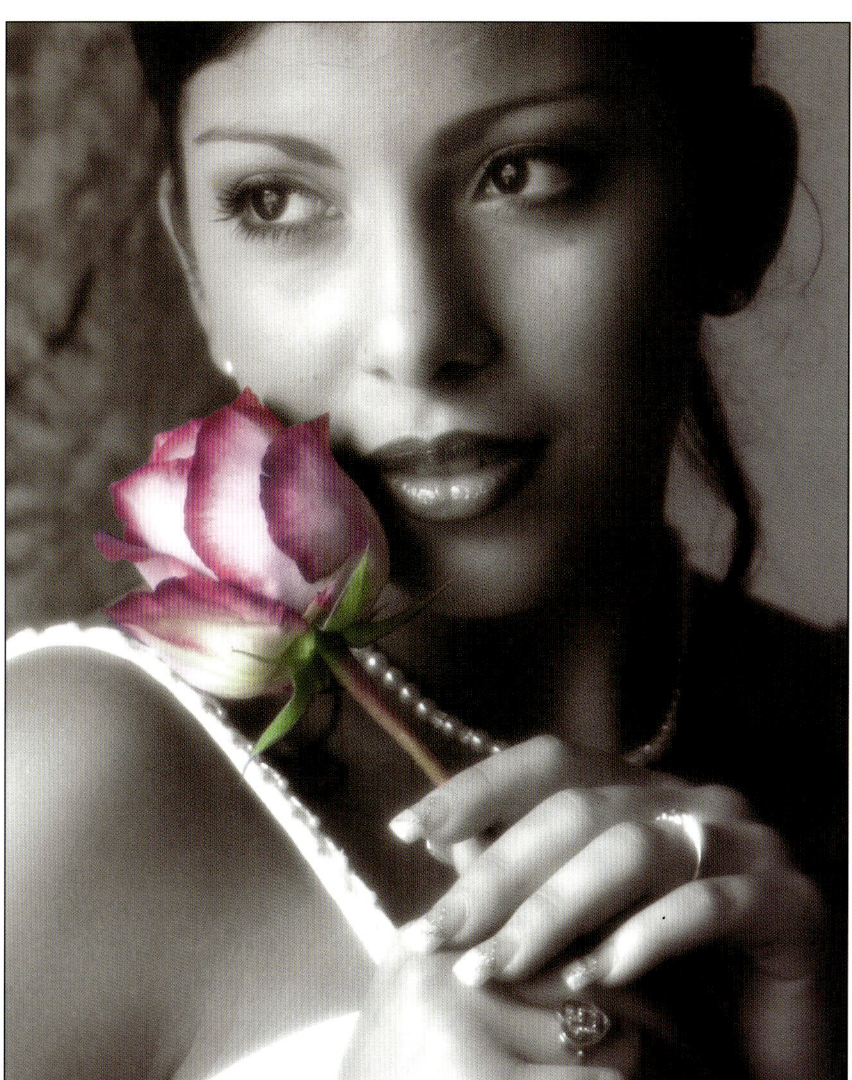
Photo by G. Rodriguez.

▶ OPTIONAL BORDER

Here is a quick way to add a colored border around your logo. These steps assume you are continuing on from step 11 in the previous example (and that you did not decide to flatten the image file).

Step 1—Activate the background layer by clicking on it in the Layers palette.

Step 2—Select the entire image by going to Select>All.

Step 2—Apply a stroke to the selection (this is a line around a selection). To do this, go to Edit>Stroke. In the dialog box, set the width as you like. Click on the color box to open the Color Picker and select the color you want. Then, click the Inside radio button to make the full width of the stroke appear within your selected area. Hit OK.

▶ CREATING THUMBNAIL IMAGES FOR A GALLERY SLIDE SHOW

A thumbnail is a small version of an image that is used as a hyperlink to show the full-size image. In this section, we will look at two different method you can use to create thumbnail images. The first method is to simply shrink the entire image to a size that is about 100 pixels high. The second method is to select an interesting portion of the full size image and crop it to the thumbnail size. The second method generates interest by enticing the viewer to enlarge the image to see it in its entirety. It is important to make all of your thumbnails the same height (100 pixels) so your gallery page will have a uniform look.

Generate interest by enticing the viewer to enlarge the image to see it in its entirety.

We'll also take the time during this process to set up your images as you'll need them to use in your gallery slide show (see chapter 4 for more on this topic).

Method #1: Shrink the Entire Image

Step 1—From the File menu choose Open. From the dialog box that appears, select the image file to open and then click OK.

Step 2—Next, you must optimize your file resolution for Internet use. To do this, go to the Image menu and choose Image Size. In the Image Size dialog box type 72 in the Resolution window and choose pixels/inch from the resolution drop-down menu. Click OK.

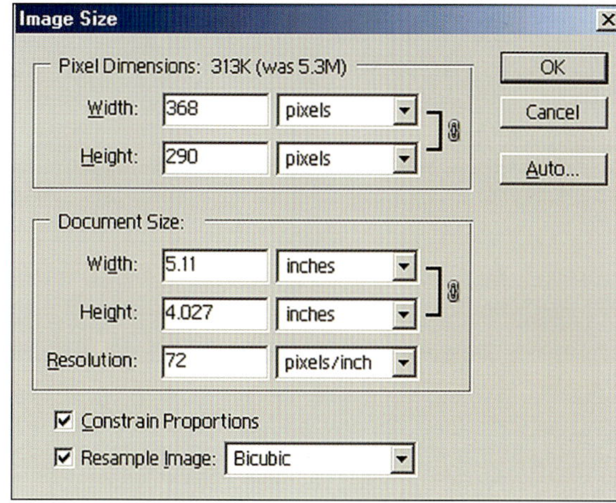

Figure 3-55

Step 3—Perform any needed photo optimizations (i.e. cropping, adjusting brightness, any Photoshop editing). Next, we'll set up your image as you'll need it for use in your slide-show display. From the Image menu choose Image Size. In the Image Size dialog box, check the Constrain Proportions box and check the Resample Image box. Set the height of the image to 350 pixels and click OK. If your photo is less than 300–350 pixels to begin with, you should re-scan the photo to a higher magnification. The photos in the gallery template (see chapter 4) are 400 pixels wide.

Step 4—From the File menu choose Save As. Give your edited image a unique name and save it in the JPG file format. Create a folder named "Pictures" to save the full size image. For convenience and future reference, save your thumbnails in a separate folder named "Thumbnails." (It is a good practice to give your gallery images a common name then add a numeral at the end of each. For instance pic01.jpg, pic02.jpg, pic03.jpg and so on will help you organize your gallery and your slide show. In the JPEG dialog box, choose a low- to medium-quality file size. At the bottom of the JPEG dialog box, you'll see a section called "Size" that offers an estimate of the load time at different modem speeds. Most computers with dial-up connections are equipped with 56.6bps modems, so choose this speed to get an estimate of load time for your image (Figure 3-55).

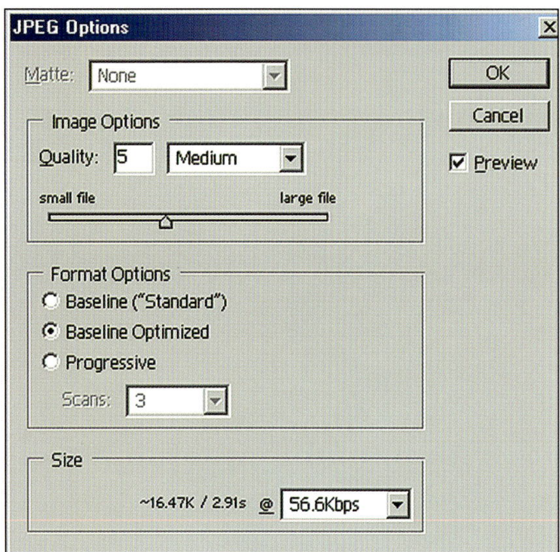

Figure 3-55

Step 5—Now you can resize your image as a thumbnail. From the Image menu choose Image Size. In the Image Size dialog box, check the Constrain Proportions and Resample Image boxes. Then, set the height of the image to 100 pixels and click OK.

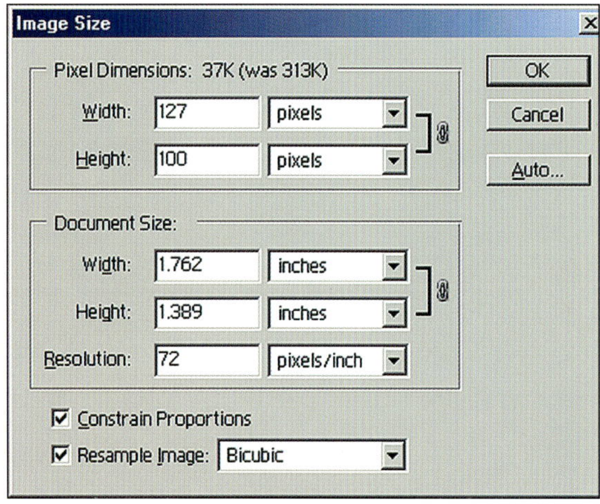

Figure 3-56

Step 6—From the File menu choose Save As and name the new image. It's helpful to give related names to each thumbnail and its corresponding full-size image. Using the same numeric ending in their names is a good way to accomplish this. For example the full size image pic01.jpg will correspond with the small image thumb01.jpg, and the full size image pic02.jpg will correspond with the small image thumb02.jpg, and so on. Save the thumbnail at a low-quality file size in the JPEG Options window.

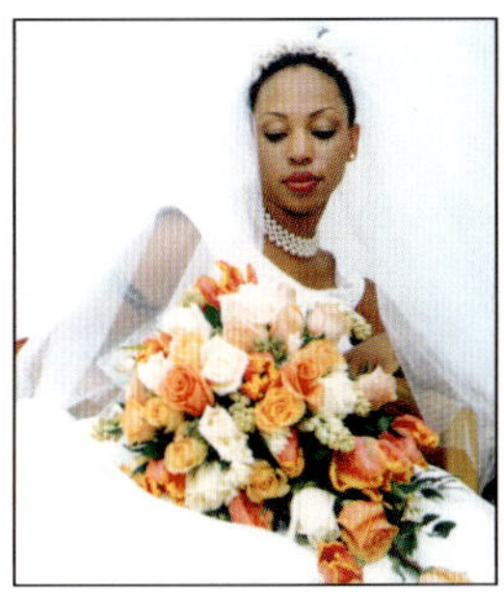

Figure 3-57: Thumbnail (above) and full image (right). Photograph by Bob Tancott.

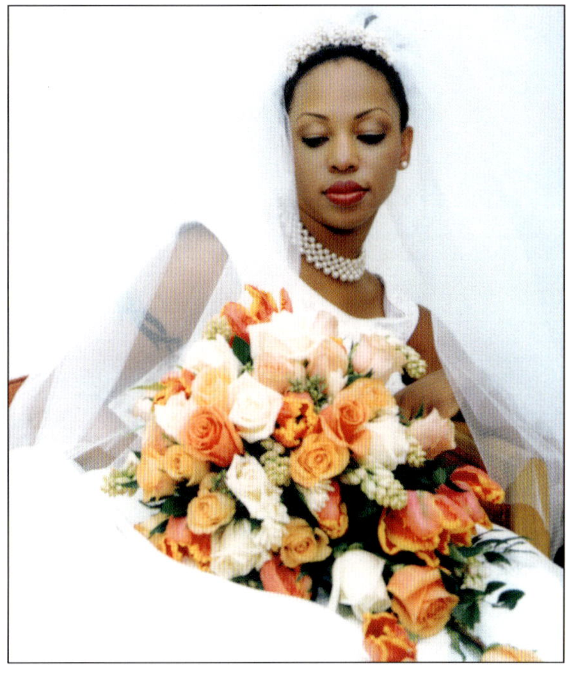

Method #2: Cut Out a Square Portion of the Image

Step 1—From the File menu choose Open. From the dialog box, select the image file to open and then click OK.

Step 2—To begin, you need to optimize your file resolution for Internet use. From the Image menu choose Image Size. In the Image Size dialog box, set the resolution to 72 pixels/inch. Click OK.

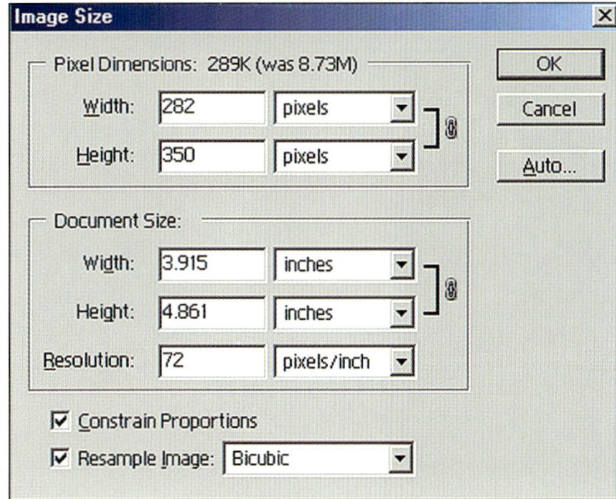

Figure 3-58

Step 3—Perform any needed photo optimizations (i.e. cropping, adjusting brightness, any Photoshop editing). Next, we'll set up your image as you'll need it for use in your slide-show display. From the Image menu choose Image Size. In the Image Size dialog box, check the Constrain Proportions box and check the

Resample Image box. Set the height of the image to 350 pixels and click OK. If your photo is less than 300–350 pixels to begin with, you should re-scan the photo to a higher magnification. The photos in the gallery template (see chapter 4) are 400 pixels wide.

Step 4—From the File menu choose Save As. Give your edited image a unique name and save it in the JPG file format. (For tips on naming and saving your slide-show images and thumbnails, see page 59.)

Step 5—Select the Crop tool from the Toolbox. In the Options bar at the top of the screen, enter 100 pixels for height and 100 pixels for width.

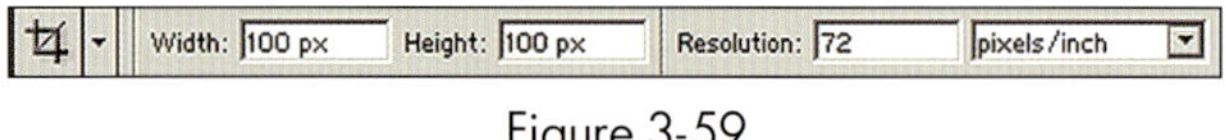

Figure 3-59

Locate an area of the image that will generate interest and entice the viewer. Place the cursor in the upper left corner of your chosen area. Click and drag the cursor diagonally to the bottom right corner of your chosen area (Figure 3-60) and release the mouse button. Double-click inside the crop area to complete the resizing (Figure 3-61).

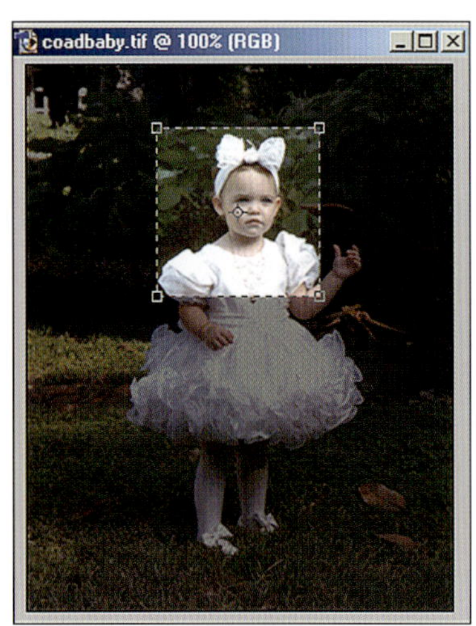

Figure 3-60

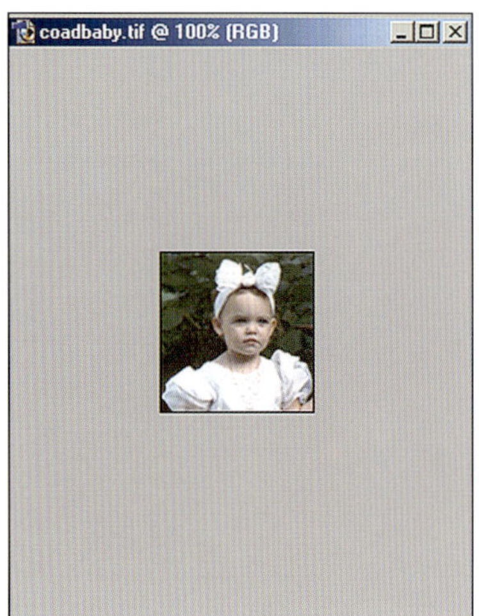

Figure 3-61

Step 6—From the File menu, choose Save As and name the new image. Again, it's a good idea to choose image names for your thumbnails that relate them to the full-size image for the gallery slide show (see page 66). Save the thumbnail at a low quality file size in the JPG dialog box.

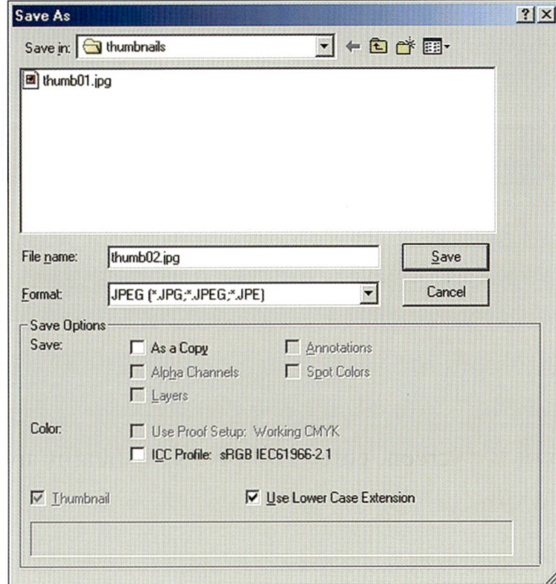

Figure 3-62

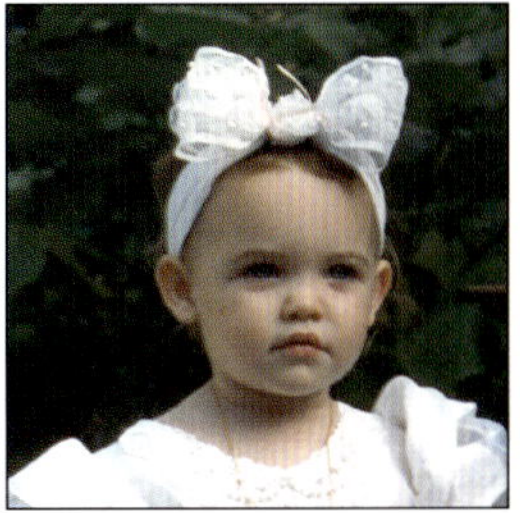

Figure 3-63: Thumbnail (above) and full image (right). Photograph by Richard Cyril Coad.

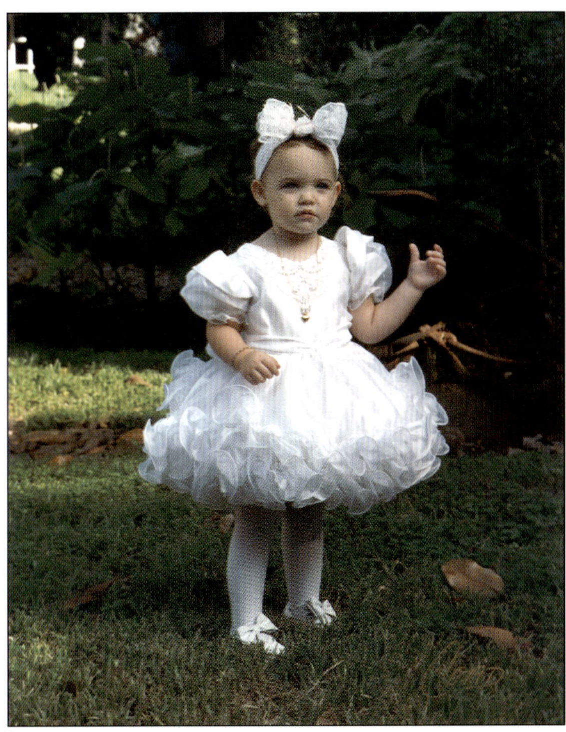

► CREATING A PHOTO COLLAGE

A photo collage is a popular method for artistically displaying a group of favorite images or to create a storytelling effect. In this section, you will select some favorite images and combine them into a single picture that is layered and features a shadow effect. You should perform your Photoshop editing of each image and save it prior to beginning the photo collage sequence described here. Select one image to be the focal point of the collage; the other images will contribute to the overall effect of the collage. Choose different sizes and shapes to add interest to your collage.

Step 1—Begin by opening all of the images that you plan to use in your collage. For each image, adjust the resolution and image size. The resolution should be 72 pixels/inch and the image size will vary depending on whether the photograph is to be the focal point image or one of the supporting images. You may wish to start with images that are about 200–300 pixels in height or width—you can change these as your collage takes shape. To size your images, go to the Image menu and select Image Size. In the dialog box, set the resolution to 72 pixels/inch and set the width or height to approximately 200–300 pixels.

Step 2—From the File menu select New. Set the width to 750 pixels, the height to 400 pixels , the resolution to 72 pixels/inch, the mode to RGB, and the contents to white. Click OK. Set the window view to 80% so you see the entire window without scrolling (you can do this with the Zoom tool or by entering 80% in the box at the lower left corner of the image window). This will be the window in which you create your collage.

Step 3—Click and drag each image into the collage window. To adjust the size of an image, click on the image layer in the Layers palette, then go to Edit>Transform>Scale. When the bounding box appears, click and drag the handles to re-size the image. Holding down the Shift key as you do this will maintain the aspect ratio and prevent your image from becoming distorted (Figure 3-64).

Step 4—To move an image, click on the image layer in the Layers palette, then select the Move tool and reposition the image by clicking and dragging it (Figure 3-65).

Step 5—You can determine which image overlaps the others by arranging the order of the layers in the Layers palette.

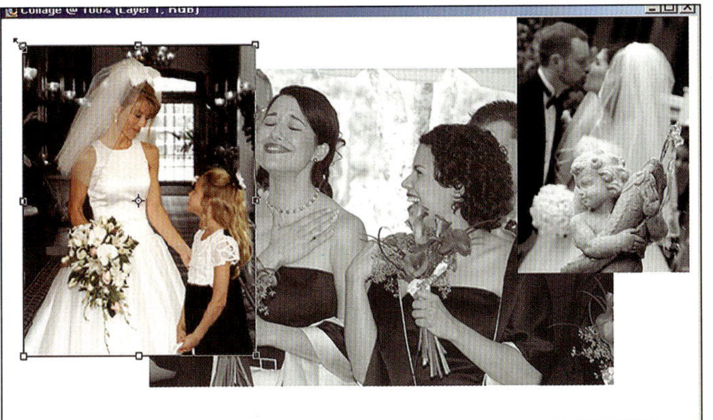

Figure 3-64

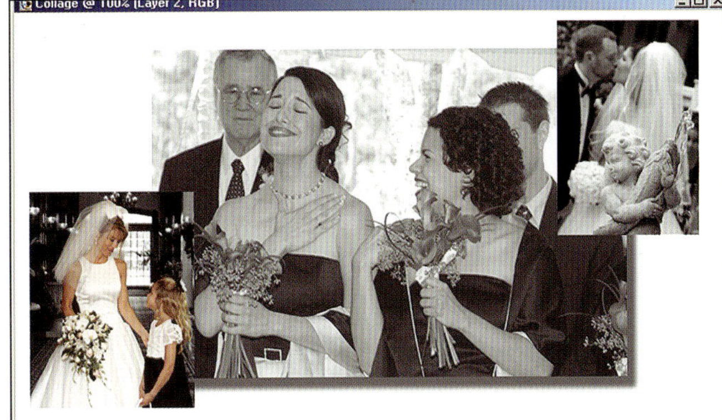

Figure 3-65

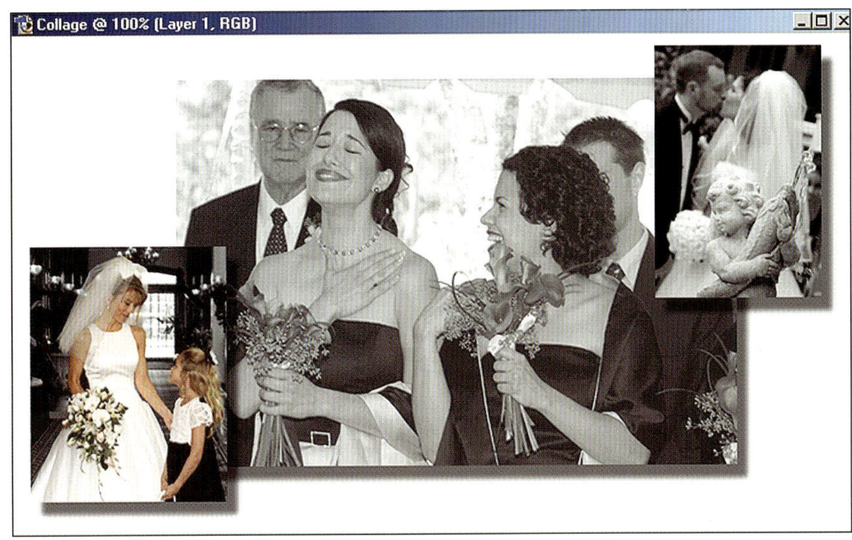

Figure 3-66: Final collage. Photography by Derek Smith.

Step 6—Once the images are in their final placement, select the first layer to which you will add the drop shadow effect. Next, go to the Layers menu and select Layer Style. Then choose Drop Shadow. In the dialog box, adjust the shadow effect options and click OK.

Step 7—Next, copy the shadow effect of this layer to all other image layers. To do this, go to the Layers palette and click on the layer with the shadow. Go to Layers>Layer Style and choose Copy Layer Style. Click on each additional layer, then go to Layers>Layer Style and choose Paste Layer Style. That completes the photo collage. Save your picture as a JPG format file with a low to medium quality for Internet use. You may wish to flatten the image (Layer>Flatten Image) to reduce the file size.

4. gallery display

In this chapter, several techniques will be demonstrated for displaying your finest images.

The first method is a thumbnail gallery page that uses a pop-up window to display an enlarged version of the selected thumbnail. The beauty of this method is the viewer can see all of your images at a glance in thumbnail size, or opt to take a closer look at enlargements with a single mouse click. This puts the user in complete control.

Pop-Up Window—A pop-up window is a separate and independent browser window in which enlarged images may be displayed. These enlarged images correspond to thumbnail images on the independent browser window.

The second method is what we call a the photojournalism collage gallery. This gallery type is popular with many photographers because of the storytelling effect that blends perfectly with the art of photojournalism.

The third method is the instructional gallery. This gallery is useful for on-line teaching of photography techniques. This gallery features images from the master's class presented by Master Photographer, Rick Ferro during a recent WPPI (Wedding and Portrait Photographers International) convention.

THUMBNAIL TO SLIDE SHOW GALLERY

The organization of your file system is the most important step for this image display method. First create a folder named gallery. Inside of the gallery folder create three other folders named thumbnails, pictures, and pages. When you create the album page save it in the gallery folder. Your filing system for the gallery display should look like Figure 4-1.

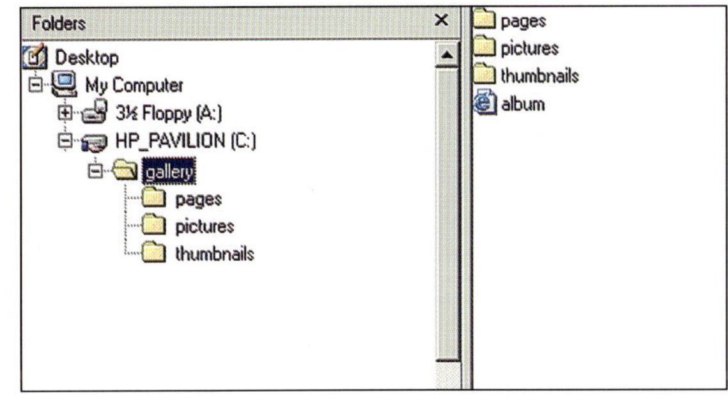

Figure 4-1: The filing system for the gallery.

Using the Downloadable Template

A gallery template is available in the materials that can be downloaded to accompany this book (see page 11). If you have downloaded these materials and will be using this template, perform the following steps to customize it. If you prefer to build your own gallery, please skip ahead to the next section.

Step 1—Select fifteen of your favorite images to use in your photo gallery. Use the Photoshop methods described in chapter 3 to size your photos and create your thumbnails. Make your photos a maximum 400 pixels tall and/or wide; make your thumbnails 100x100 pixels.

Step 2—Save your photo files in the "Pictures" folder; name them pic01, pic02, etc. as shown in Figure 4-2.

Step 3—Replace the files in the pictures folder with your own images—remember that your photos need to have the same name as those already in the folder (i.e. pic01, pic02, etc.), and they must be JPG format. The web pages found in the template reference the pictures by name, and therefore the names of the pictures must not be changed.

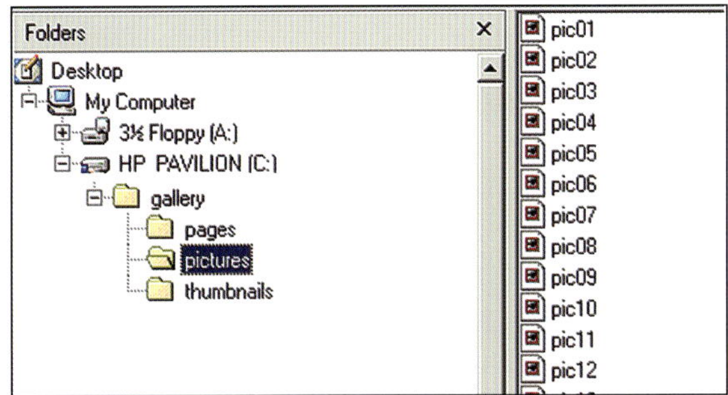

Figure 4-2: Picture folder and files.

Step 4—Save your thumbnails in the thumbnail folder; name them thumb01, thumb02, etc. as shown in Figure 4-3.

Step 5—Replace the files in the thumbnails folder. Remember your thumbnails need to have the same name as those already in the folder, i.e. thumb01, thumb02, etc, and they must be JPG format. Again, the web pages found in the template will reference the thumbnails by name, so the names of the thumbnails must be identical.

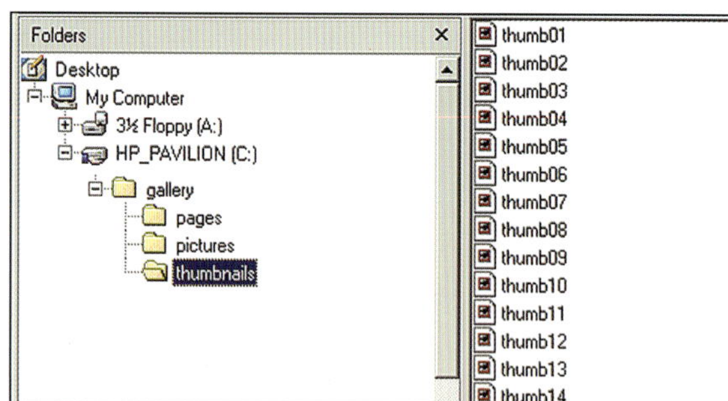

Figure 4-3:Thumbnail folder and files.

You are now finished and you have a working gallery with your own images. To test your gallery, find the file named "Album" in the gallery folder. Double click on the file name to open it. The album page will appear in your browser. Click on the thumbnails to start the slide show.

Making Your Own Template

If you prefer to make your own pages, you can create them using web page software like FrontPage. For a full discussion of creating and using tables, see chapter 5.

Step 1—Create a table with three equal columns and two rows—one large row at the top for the photo and one small one at the bottom for the text. Center the table on the page. Merge the top row of columns into one cell to accommodate the single photo. Insert your first image (pic01) in the merged cell. Type "< back" in the bottom left cell and "forward >" in the bottom right cell (the bottom center cell is used as a spacer). Your page should look like Figure 4-4. Save this page in the pages folder, and name it page01.

Table—A rectangle divided into sections using vertical and horizontal lines. The small boxes defined by the horizontal and vertical lines are called "cells" The group of cells that stack horizontally are called "columns." The group of cells that align vertically are called "rows."

Cells—In a table, the small boxes defined by the horizontal and vertical lines.

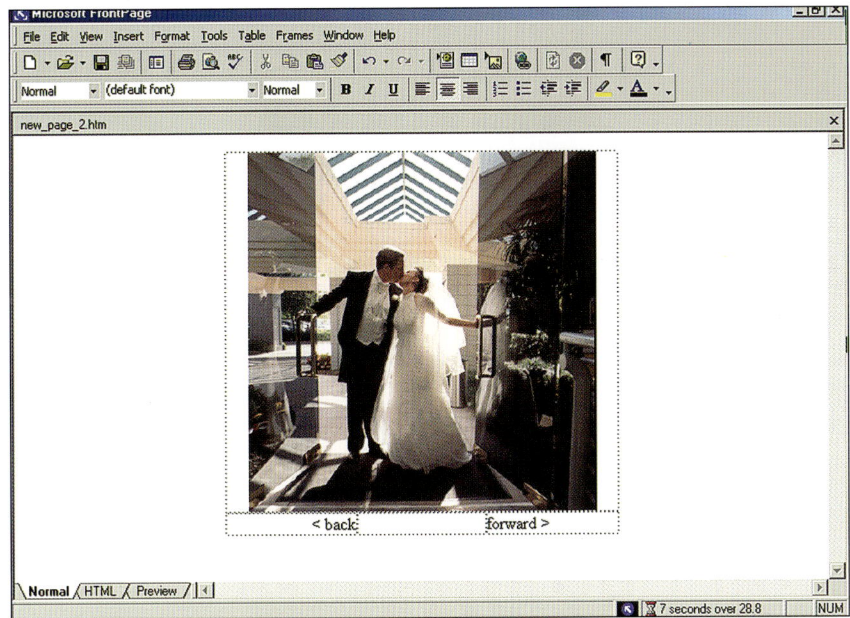

Figure 4-4: The pop-up page created using FrontPage software.

Step 2—Continue making pages this way—one page per image—by inserting the remaining images (pic02, pic03, etc.) in the top cell of the table, and then saving the updated pages with unique file names that place them in numerical order (page02, page03, etc.). Your "Pages" folder will contain all the pages as shown in Figure 4-6.

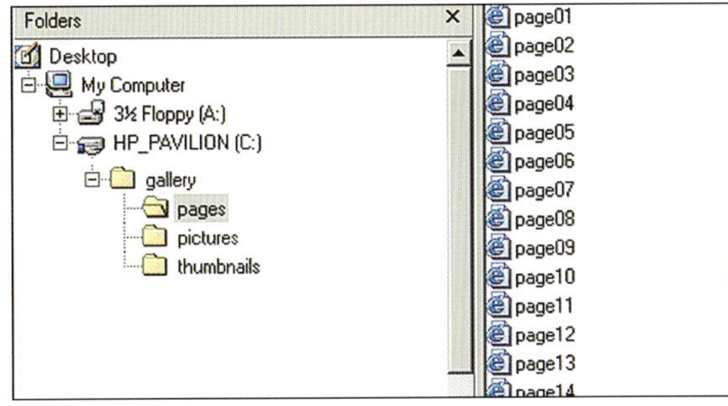

Figure 4-5: Pages folder.

Step 3—Next, you'll need to create a thumbnail gallery page as shown in Figure 4-6. To do this, make a table with three rows and five columns. In each cell, place a thumbnail image in numerical order. Start at the top left then work to the right and down until each cell contains a unique thumbnail. Save this page in the "Gallery" folder and name it "Album."

Step 4—Select each thumbnail and hyperlink it to the page that corresponds with the thumbnail. For example the thumbnail

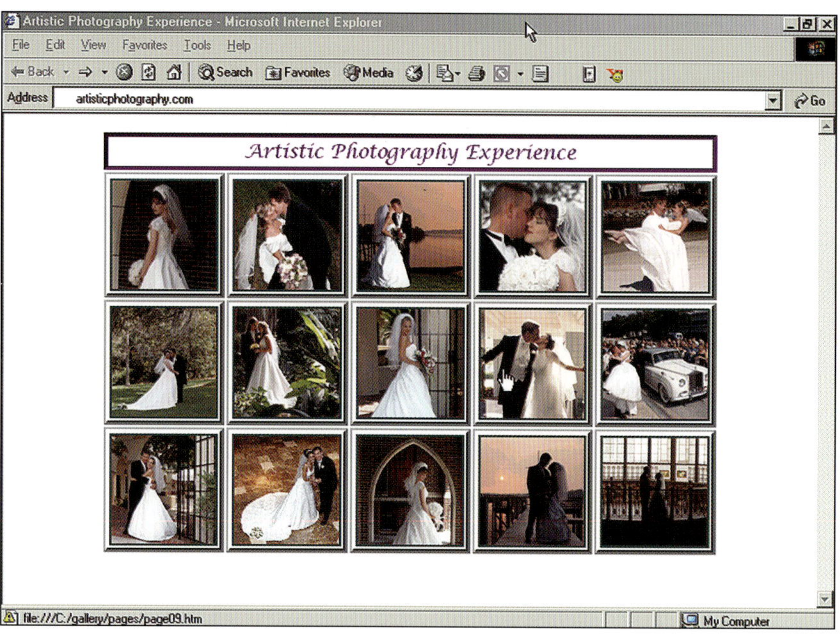

Figure 4-6: Screen shot of thumbnail gallery. Photography by Rhett Pyle.

named "thumb01" links to "page01" that has "pic01" displayed on the page. Continue until each thumbnail is linked to the proper page.

Step 5—To get the slide show to display in a pop-up window requires a few lines of JavaScript to be placed in the HTML code of the album web page. If you are not familiar with this you can look at the web page album from the template, locate the code to copy and paste it into your page. Type the following text into the header of your HTML code:

```
<head>
<SCRIPT LANGUAGE="JAVASCRIPT">
   function openwin()
  {
window.open("", "gallerypage", "toolbar=no,
left='1', top='1', location=no, status=no, menubar=no,
scrollbars=no, resizable=no, width=450,
height=450");
}
</SCRIPT>
</head>
```

→ Header—The opening section of HTML code on a web page. Set off by the opening tag "<head>" and the closing tag "</head>".

Warning! Improper source code editing can damage the function and appearance of your web site. If you are not fully confidant of your abilities, you should consult a professional web master to make these changes.

With this text you have instructed the viewer's browser to create a new window. You have named this window "gallerypage." You have also specified the features of the new window (like its width and height).

Step 6—In the following step you will direct your gallery pages to be displayed in this new window. The hyperlinks you created for each thumbnail (in step 4) each need a line of JavaScript added that will refer to the code you just inserted in step 5. In the HTML code of your album page locate the hyperlink text that looks like this line.

```
<a href="pages/page01.htm" ><img src="thumb-
nails/thumb01.jpg" width="100" height="100"></a>
```

Change the line by adding the text shown in red. This must be done for each of the fifteen lines of code that link the thumbnails to the pages.

```
<a href="pages/page01.htm" onclick="openwin()"
target="gallerypage"><img
src="thumbnails/thumb01.jpg" width="100"
height="100"></a>
```

Your new album page is now complete. Save it in the "Gallery" folder.

Step 7—The final requirement for completing your slide show is linking the individual slide-show pages backward and forward. To do this, open the file "page01" in your web page software. Hyperlink the word "forward" to go to "page02." Remove the word "back" since this is your first page. Save and close the page.

Step 8—Open the file "page02." Hyperlink the word "forward" to go to "page03." Hyperlink the word "back" to go to "page01." Save and close this page. Continue this process with each additional page linking "back" to the previous page and "forward" to the next page. When you arrive at the final page ("page15") remove the word "forward," since this is your last page.

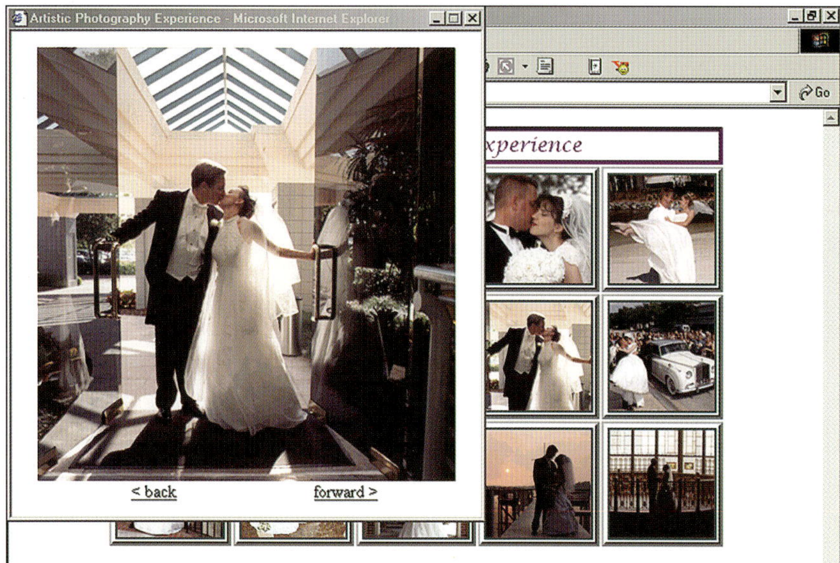

Figure 4-7: Pop-up enlargement from the thumbnail gallery.

Your gallery and slide-show presentation are now complete. To test your slide show open the album page in your browser, then click on each thumbnail to verify that the correct page is displayed. Run through your slide show forward and backward to test the links. Using a Microsoft Explorer browser, your slide show should appear as in Figure 4-7. You may also wish to preview your web site using other popular browsers, such as Netscape, to ensure all viewers will be able to view it accurately.

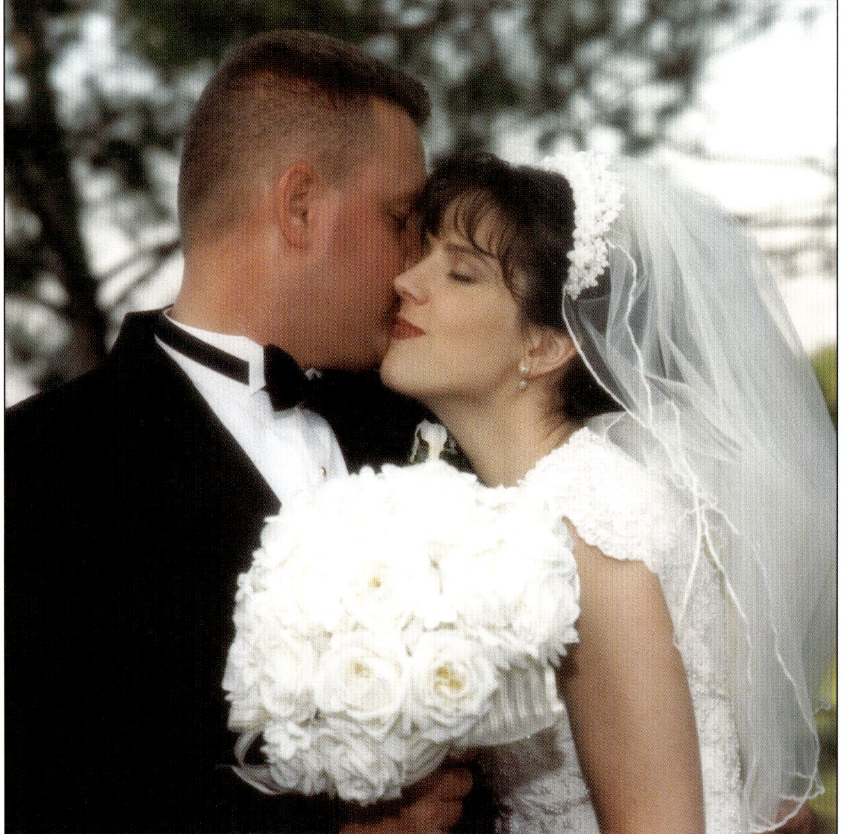

Photograph by Rhett Pyle.

The viewer is immediately drawn to the entire display, thus creating a storytelling effect.

PHOTOJOURNALISM COLLAGE GALLERY

Computers provide a new lease on life for photojournalism. The marriage of words and pictures that exists in print can now be transposed to this electronic medium. Far from being an outmoded form of communication, the need and demand for quality professional photojournalism is greater than ever.

Photojournalistic images are viewed as art pieces. By using a photo collage gallery, the viewer is immediately drawn to the entire display, thus creating a storytelling effect. The collage is a popular choice for many photographers.

Gary Fox, a top wedding photojournalist from central Florida, provides the following tips. "As a wedding photojournalist, the first rule is to become aware of the emotion happening all around, and being prepared to react instantly. This requires the correct tools. As the events at the wedding unfold, the perfect shot may be two feet in front of me, or seventy-five feet away. I must be ready to get the shot at the exact moment it happens or it is gone forever. I am normally outfitted with three Canon EOS-1n camera bodies with lenses ranging from a 15mm fisheye to a 350mm telephoto."

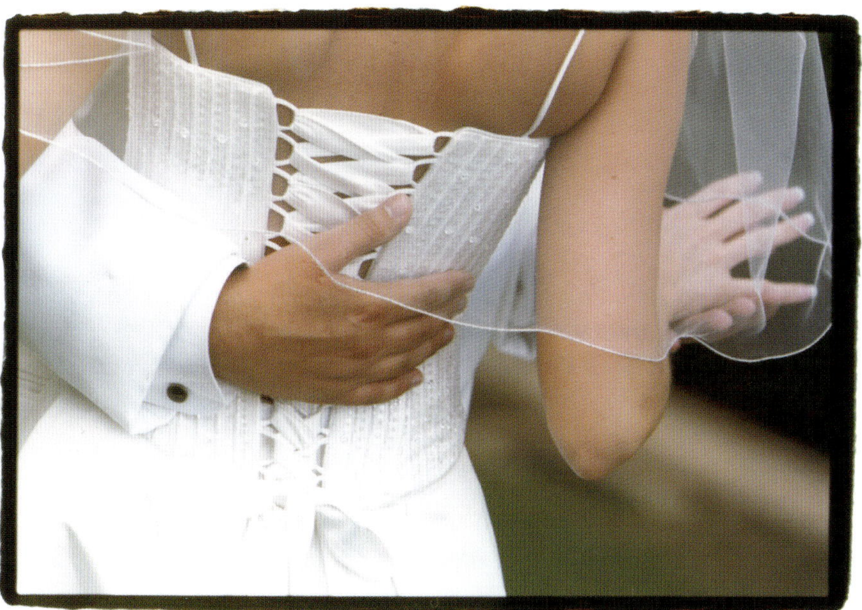

Figure 4-8: The magic of photojournalism. Photography by Gary Fox.

When placing your images in the photo collage, it is wise to group them into subtopics. For instance, in the collage displayed in Figure 4-7 there are four groupings of images. The subtopics are: the bride, the groom, the champagne toast, and the dance. Grouping photos improves the storytelling effect of your collage.

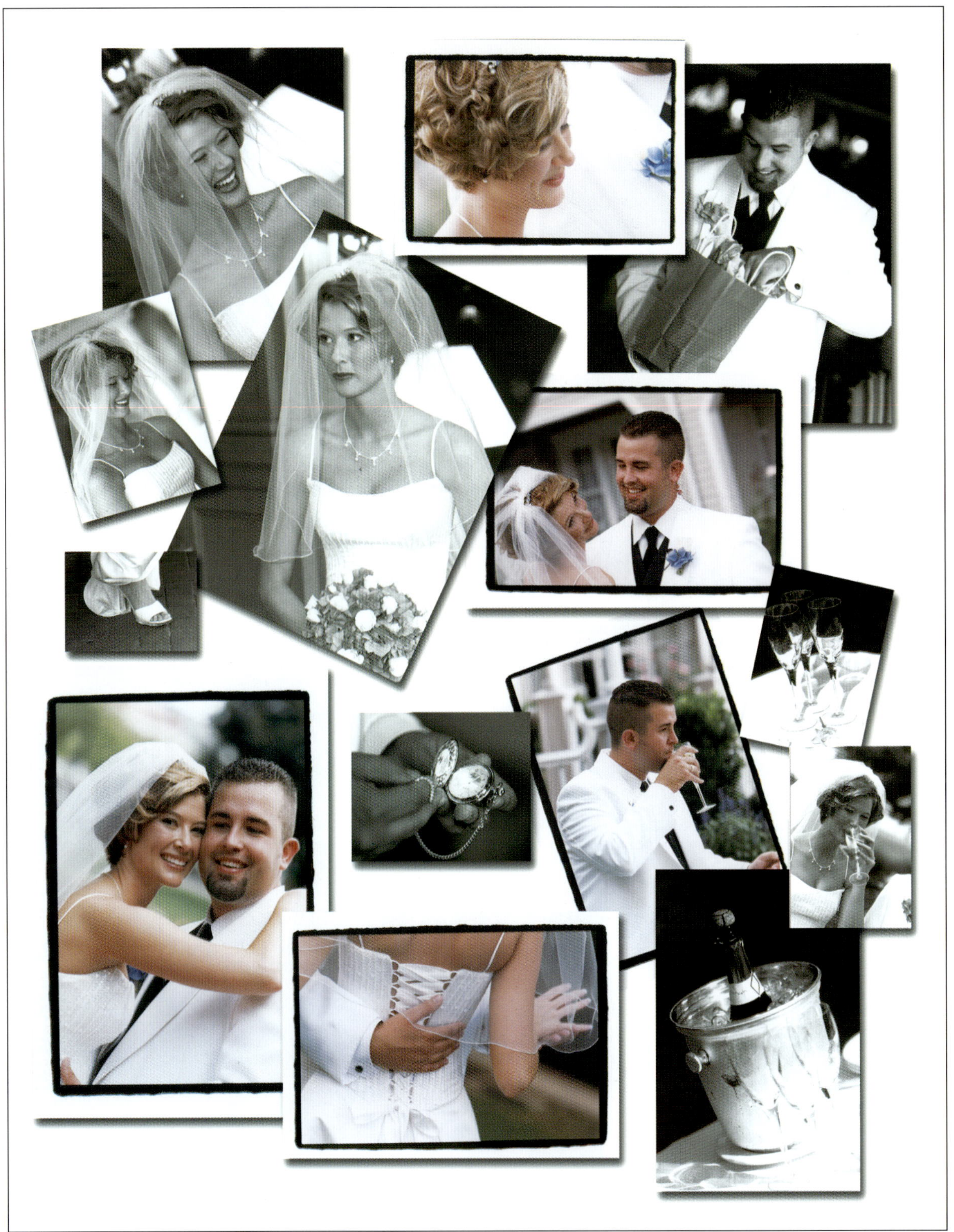

Figure 4-9: The completed collage contains subgroups for storytelling effect. Photography by Gary Fox.

You should prepare your collage using Photoshop software as described in chapter 3. Save your image as a low- to medium-quality JPG file to minimize the file size and reduce the load time. The maximum width of your collage should be 750–800 pixels so it can be comfortably viewed on most monitors.

ON-LINE TEACHING GALLERY

Using frame pages allows the viewer to see a great deal of information at once, without having to scroll from page to page. In the next example, shown in Figure 4-10, you will see this method employed to create an on-line teaching session. Master photographer Rick Ferro's WPPI Master Class images are the subject matter, and the frame pages are developed using FrontPage software.

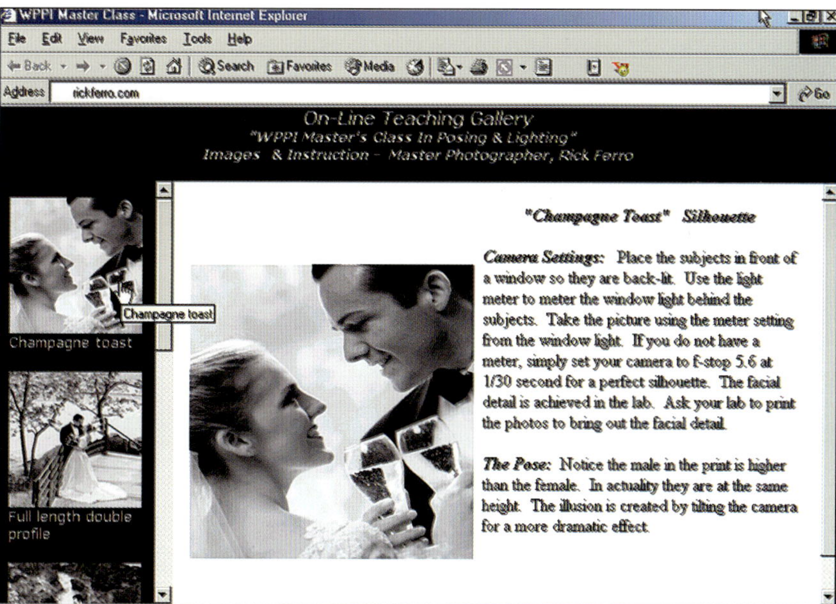

Figure 4-10: An on-line teaching gallery using frame page layout. Photography by Rick Ferro.

Frames—Devices used to divide a browser window into independent sections.

As you can see in Figure 4-10, the web page is divided into three sections called frames. The first frame runs along the top of the page and contains the title of the course. This frame is named "title." The left-hand frame contains a selection menu and is named "menu." The right-hand frame contains the instructional material and is named "instruction." The page designer names the frames.

One advantage of using frames for this type of display is the independence of each frame. For example, the menu frame contains its own scroll bar that scrolls only the menu frame. Scrolling the menu will not affect the information in the other frames. Likewise, the instruction frame is equipped with its own scrollbar for viewing the instructional material without affecting the menu frame. The title frame is a set size, so no scroll bar is required.

Another advantage of the three-frame system is the versatility of being able to call pages from one frame and have them appear in a different frame. The example shown here calls pages from the menu frame when the user makes a selection. The information then appears in the instruction frame (called the target frame). Taking this idea one step further, you might have several chapters in your on-line course. You provide a list of the chapters in the title frame, then the user selects a chapter from the list. The menu for the contents of the chapter then appears in the menu frame. When the user then chooses a topic from the menu frame, the instructional text and/or photo appears in the instruction frame.

This three-frame method actually requires four pages to make it work. The first page is called the frames page (shown in Figure 4-11). The second page is called the title page that fills the title frame shown in Figure 4-12. The third page is the menu page that fills the menu frame shown in Figure 4-13. The fourth page is the text page that fills the instruction frame shown in Figure 4-14.

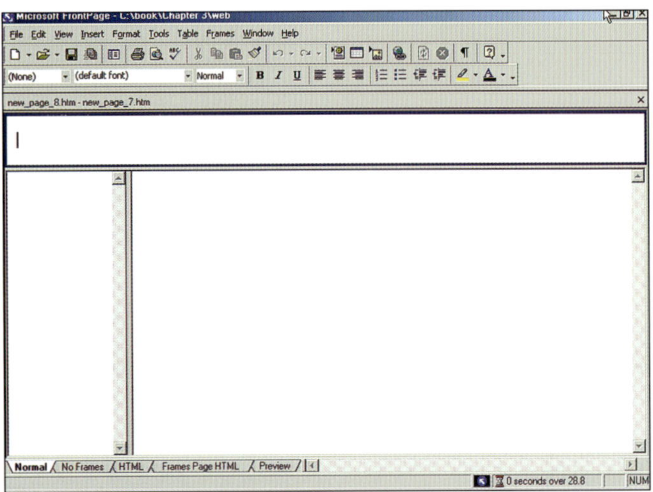

Figure 4-11:The frames page encompasses the frames.

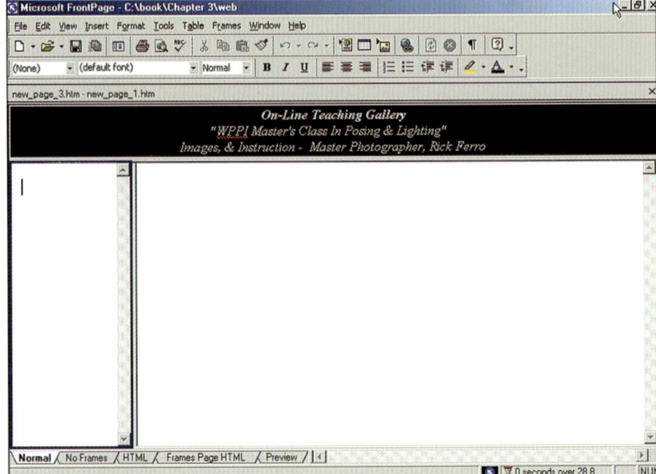

Figure 4-12: The title page fills the title frame.

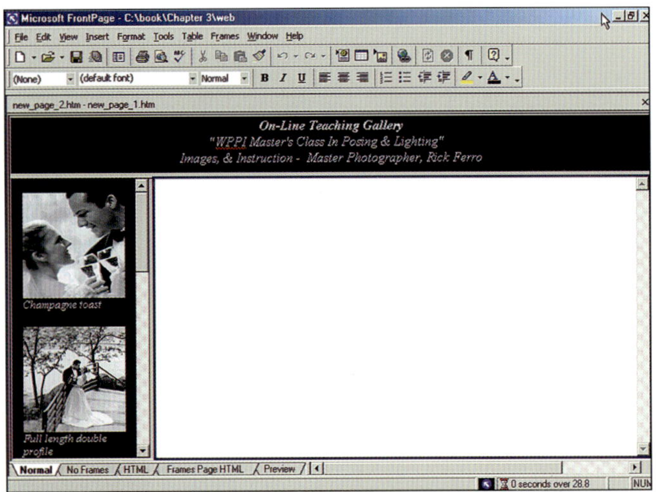

Figure 4-13:The menu page fills the menu frame.

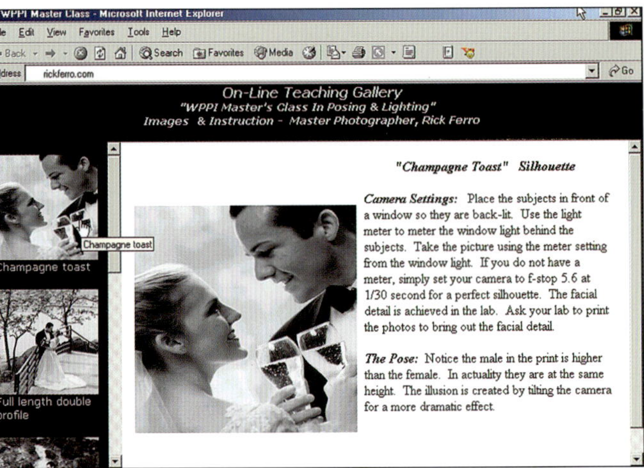

Figure 4-14: The text page fills the instruction frame.

When developing a frame page using FrontPage software you can create all of the required pages in the frame-page view. When you save your work, FrontPage prompts you to name each of the frame pages separately. Chapter 5 explains in detail how to create a frame-page gallery.

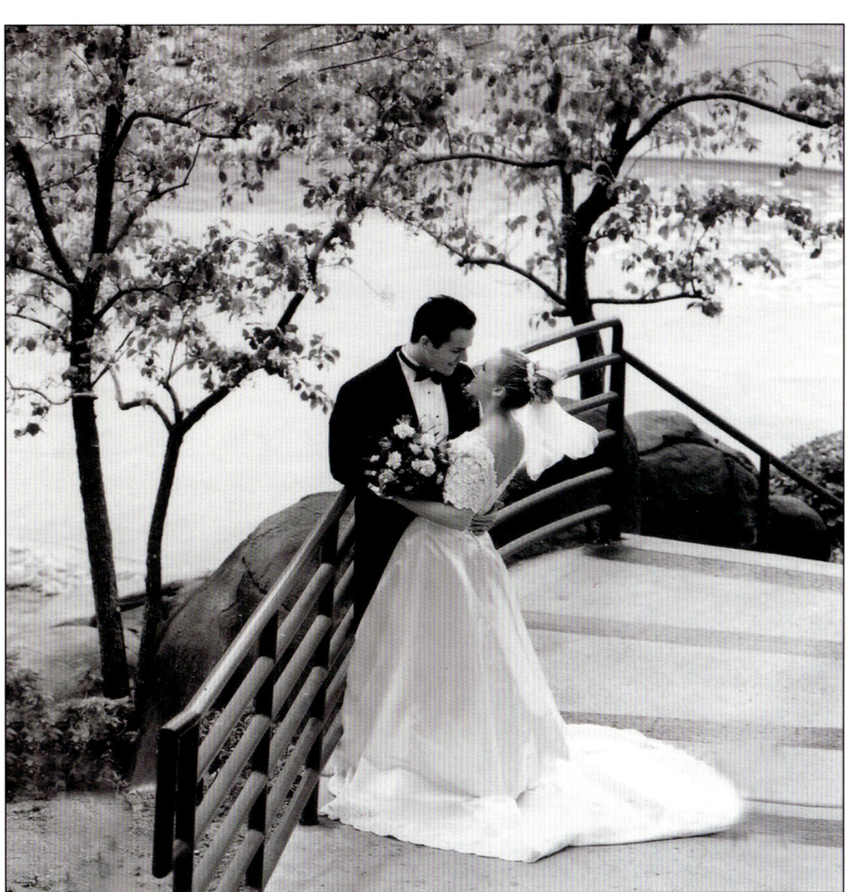

Photograph by Rick Ferro.

In this chapter, you will follow the steps needed to build a complete web site. The example demonstrates pages built using FrontPage software, but other software will yield the same results following the same general steps. Before you begin, you should select the images for your pages and prepare them using Photoshop. In this example, the web site will contain pages for various photographic services—high fashion, wedding, commercial, and sports photography.

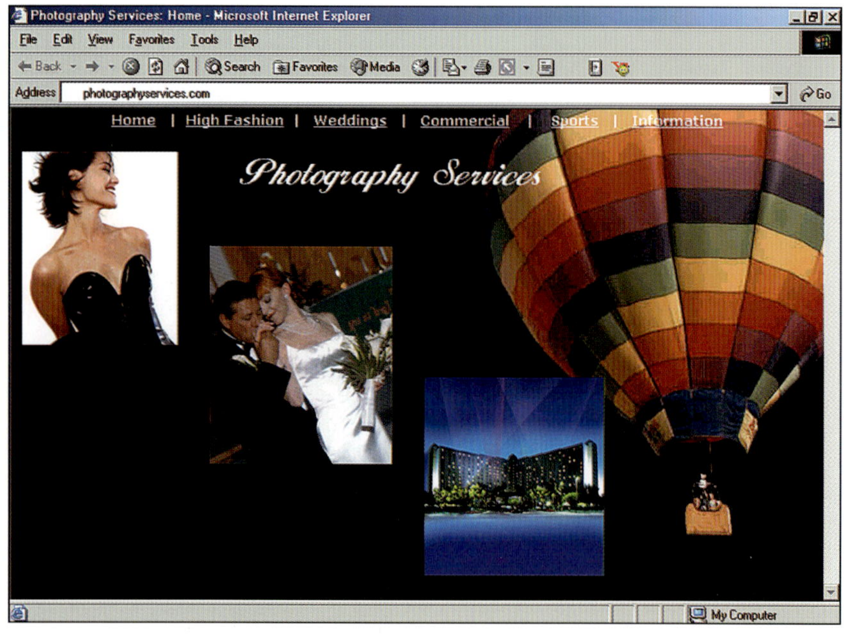

Figure 5-1: Opening page for a multi-service photography studio.

► CREATE THE WEB

FrontPage will create your folder system for the web site automatically. To begin, open the FrontPage program. From the File menu choose New and then select Web. In the dialog box, choose Empty

Web. In the Specify Location block, enter the directory path and the name for your web folder. Click OK and FrontPage will create the folder for your web site. The folder will contain a secondary folder called "images" that you can use to keep your image files separate from your page files.

A time-saving practice when developing your web site is to initially create a blank page for each of the main pages.

A time-saving practice when developing your web site is to initially create a blank page for each of the main pages of your web site. By doing this in the beginning, it is easy to make your menu bar and create the hyperlinks from page to page. You also get a clear idea of how your web site will be organized.

Step 1—To open a new page using FrontPage got to the File menu, select New, then choose Page. In the dialog box that appears, select Normal Page and click OK.

Step 2—To give the page a title, right click on the page. In the dialog box that appears, select Page Properties. Under the General tab, find the Title block and type the title of your page. The title of the page we'll be looking at is "Photography Services: Home." Click OK. Keep in mind that the title that you give your page will appear at the top of the browser window when viewed on the Internet. This is an opportunity to use the space for your phone number, city location, company name, etc.

Step 3—Saving your page is the next step. To do this, go to the File menu and select Save As. In the dialog box that appears, name the page and click Save. Follow these steps for each page of your web site. Give each page a descriptive title and name. The demonstration pages are named:

- wedding
- fashion
- commercial
- sports
- information

► SET THE HOME PAGE BACKGROUND

In this example, a balloon image is used for the page background. Using a picture in the background allows you to place other photos over it, thus creating the look of a collage.

The background picture is 800 pixels wide and 500 pixels high. If the page size exceeds the picture size the result will be an undesirable repeating of the background image as shown in Figure 5-2. When using a picture for the background be sure to size the picture to fit the page.

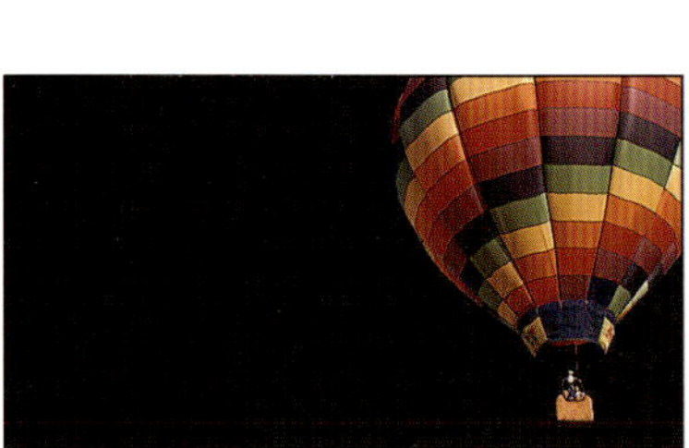

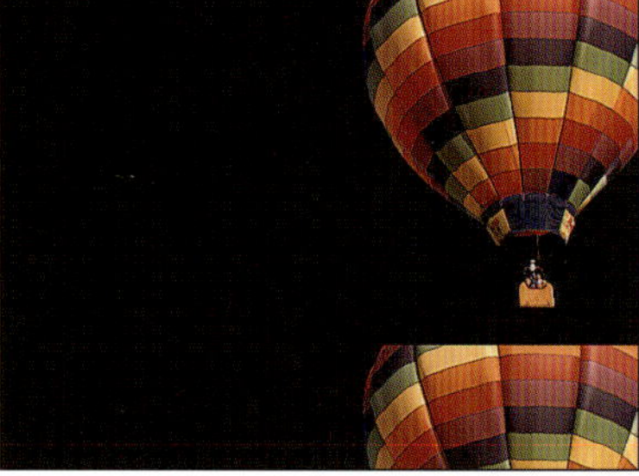

Figure 5-2: The background will repeat if the page size is larger than the background picture.

All of the pictures that you plan to use on your pages should be sized using Photoshop. Remember the resolution for the Internet is 72 pixels/inch. During the design phase, you may discover you need to resize images. Although FrontPage software and other page design software offer resizing capability, you'll find that using Photoshop will give you a much better result.

To set the properly-sized background picture in your FrontPage document, use the following procedure:

Step 1—From the Format menu choose Background (this opens the Page Properties dialog box to the Background tab). In the

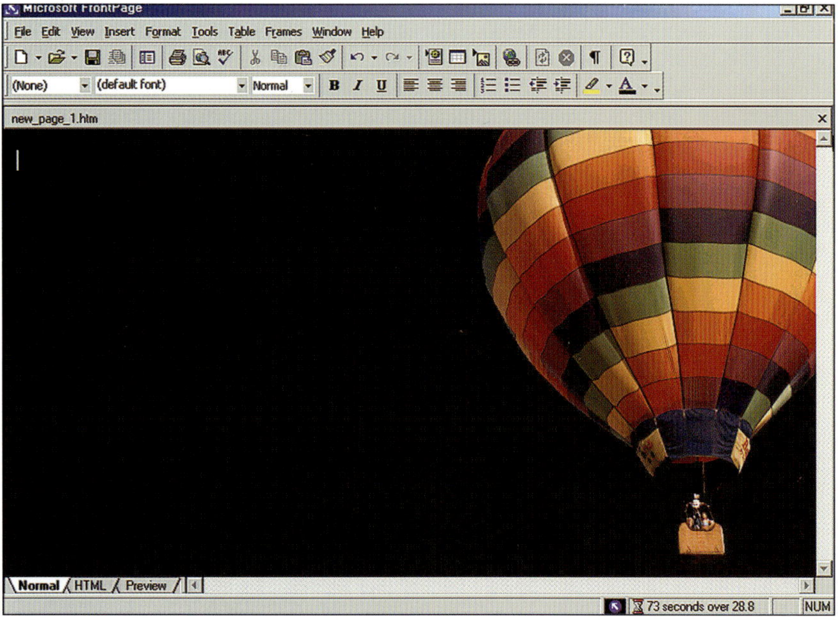

Figure 5-3: The page using the balloon image as the background image. Photography by Wayne Ebinger.

dialog box, check the Background picture box. Click on the Browse button.

Step 2—In the dialog box, locate the image file that you are using for the background, then highlight the file and click OK. The Background tab of the Page Properties dialog box also features options for other page properties. You can select the hyperlink colors at this time or return to this window later.

Step 3—Click OK to view your page with the background image (Figure 5-3).

► CREATE THE NAVIGATION MENU

In this example, a single-celled table is used as a navigation menu. Inside the table are words that link to other pages in the web site.

Step 1—From the Table menu select Insert, and then select Table. In the dialog box, make the settings as shown in Figure 5-4.

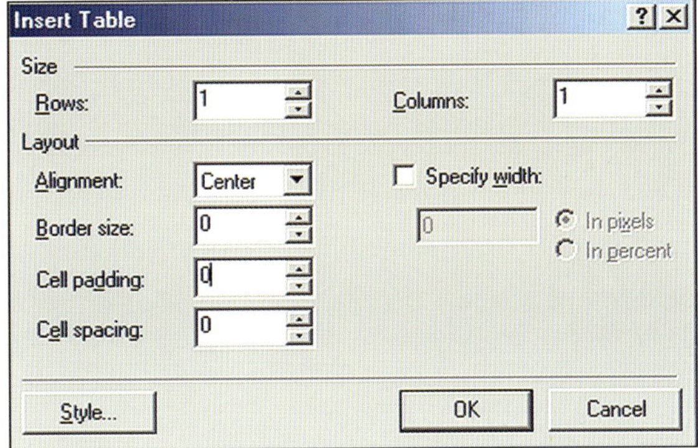

Figure 5-4: Table settings for the navigation menu.

Step 2—Place your cursor inside the table. Select a font and font color. Type the titles of the pages that will make up your web site. In this example the page titles are separated with the horizontal bar symbol "|". You may also want to include a link in this bar for e-mail (see page 83).

Step 3—The dotted line that defines the table indicates that there is no visible border around the table. If a border is desired, right click inside the table. In the pop-up menu, select Table Properties. In the Table Properties window, set the border size and color.

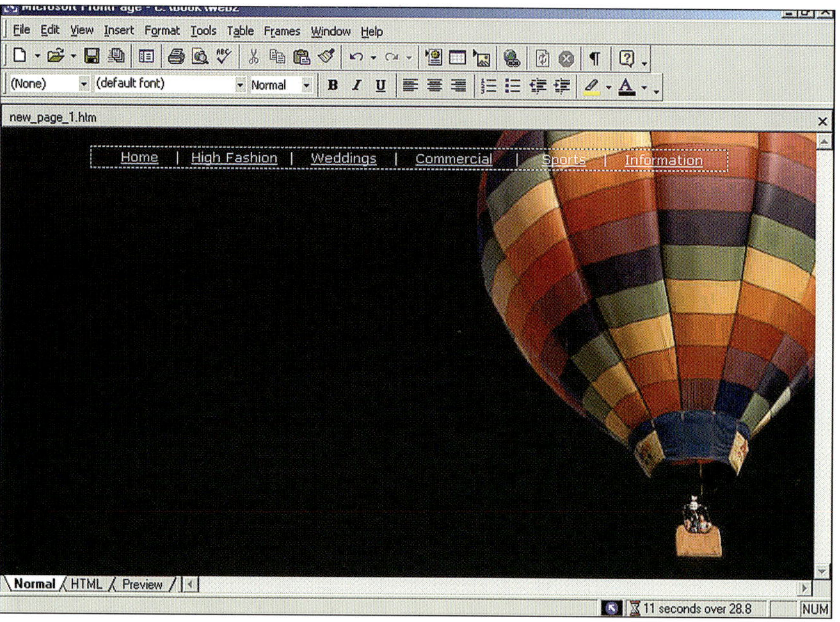

Figure 5-5: Inserting the navigation table.

Step 4—Each word in the menu bar needs to be linked to the page that it represents. Highlight one of the words (i.e. Weddings). From the Insert menu, choose Hyperlink. In the pop-up window you will see a list of the blank pages that you created earlier. Click on the page that you are linking to. In this example, the page is called "wedding.htm." The page title appears in the URL block. Click OK. The word "Wedding" in the menu bar now appears underlined. Repeat this process to link all of the words in the menu bar to their respective pages.

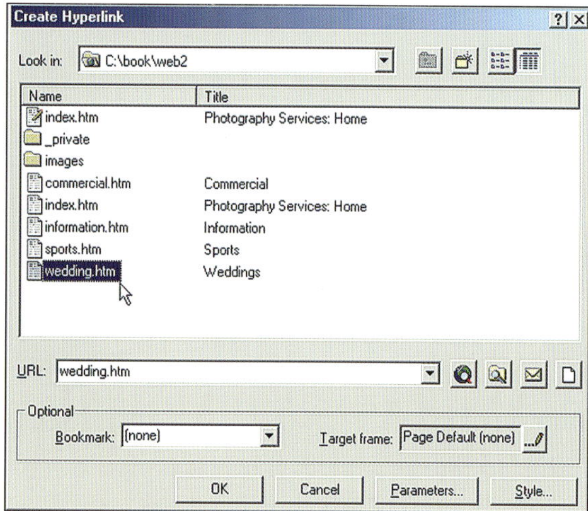

Figure 5-6: Creating a hyperlink.

► ADD AN E-MAIL LINK

You can add an e-mail link by using an e-mail button, or the word "e-mail" (creating a text link). With this method, when they click on the link, the viewer's e-mail will open with your address already inserted into the Send To block.

For a text link, as you did on page 27, highlight the word "e-mail." From the Insert menu choose Hyperlink. In the dialog box, locate the URL block. Remove everything in the block and insert the following text (using your own e-mail address, of course):

```
mailto: joe@joesdiner.com
```

► INSERT THE IMAGES

The photos to be placed over the background image can now be inserted in a new table. A table is a useful tool for positioning objects on a page. You should practice using tables and learn the methods for changing cell sizes and shapes to give your page an artistic appearance. Placing images in table cells will help give your page an organized look. Try using different placement options until you are satisfied with the overall page layout.

Step 1—Place your cursor in the last space of the table you just created and use your right arrow key to move your cursor outside of the table. Hit the enter key once.

Step 2—From the Table menu select Insert and then select Table. In the dialog box, set the new table to four rows and four columns. Set the Alignment to left and specify the Width to 80 percent as shown in Figure 5-7.

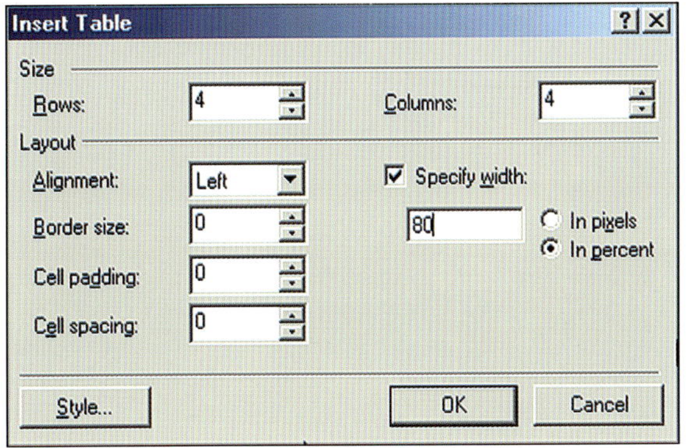

Figure 5-7: The table settings for the photo placement.

Step 3—Highlight the last three cells of the top row by clicking in one cell and dragging across the other cells. Next, right click within the highlighted area to open a dialog box and select Merge Cells.

Step 4—In the resulting cell insert the company name or logo. Select a font and font color and then type the information in the cell.

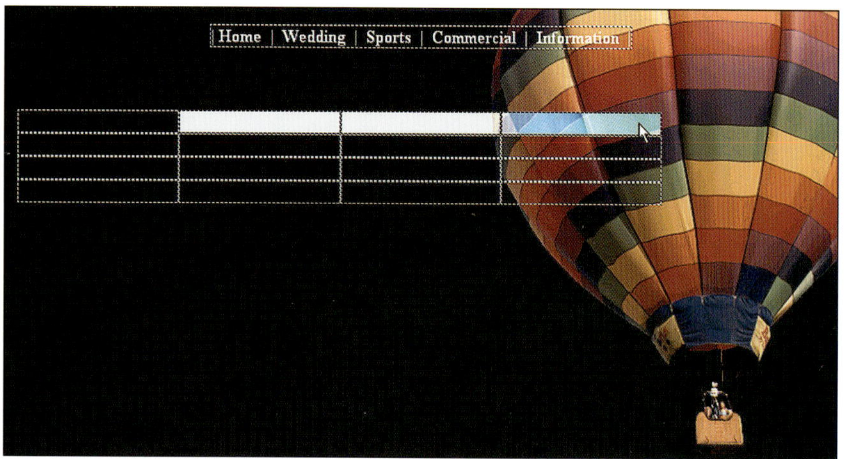

Figure 5-8: Merging cells for the Company Name.

Step 5—Next, place your cursor in the second row, second column cell. To insert an image in this cell, go to the Insert menu, select Picture, and then choose From File. In the pop-up window, locate the picture file and then click OK. Your table will look similar to Figure 5-9 (if your images are about the same size as the demonstration.)

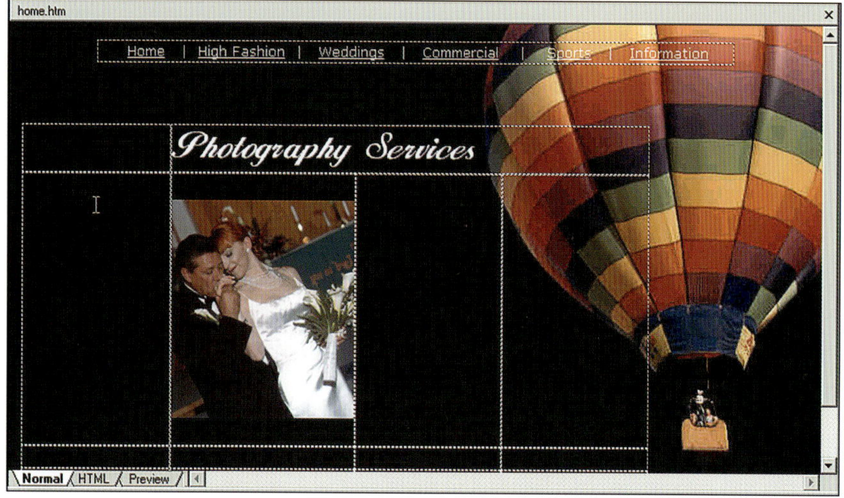

Figure 5-9: Placing the picture in the table cell. Wedding photo by J. R. Sterling.

Step 6—To add the second picture, merge the bottom three rows of the last column to make a single cell as shown in Figure 5-10. As before, insert the photo in the resulting cell. Once the photo appears in the cell, place your cursor inside the cell and right click. From the pop-up menu, select Cell Properties. In the Vertical Alignment block choose Bottom and then click OK. This step moves the picture to the bottom of the cell.

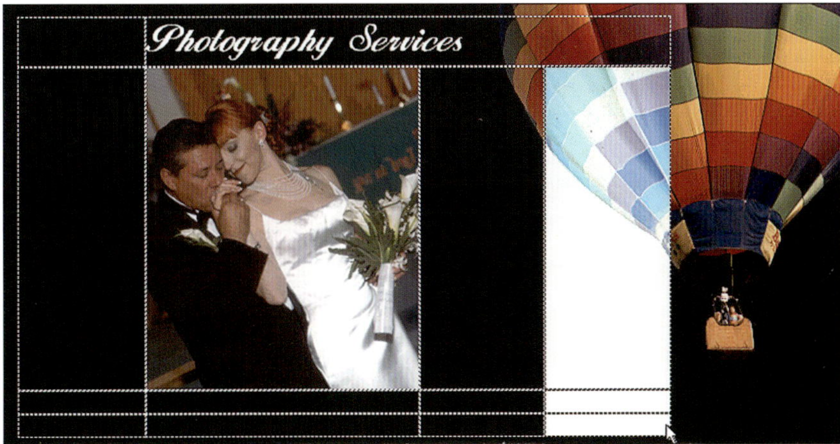

Figure 5-10: Select and merge cells for the second photo.

Step 7—To complete the table, select and merge all of the cells in the first column. Insert the final picture in the resulting cell. Once the photo appears in the cell, place your cursor inside the cell and right click. From the pop-up menu select Cell Properties. In the Vertical alignment block choose Top and then click OK. This step moves the picture to the top of the cell as shown in Figure 5-11.

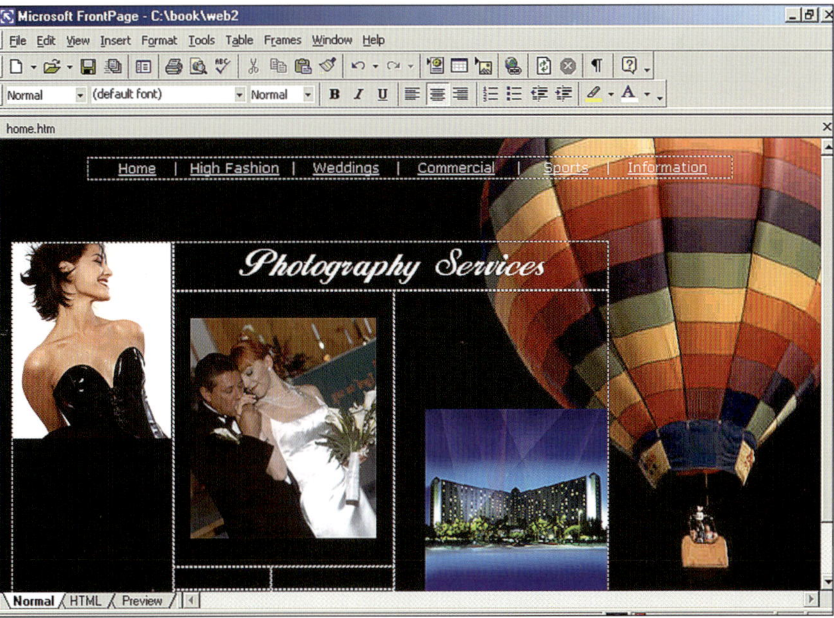

Figure 5-11: Adding the final photo to the table. Fashion photo by J. R. Sterling. Architectural photo by Richard Cyril Coad.

Step 8—FrontPage allows you to move the cell borders by placing your cursor on the border, then clicking and dragging the border to a new location. Perform these border adjustments until your table and pictures have the spacing and location that you want.

Step 9—From the File menu, select Save As. In the dialog box, select the folder and name the file "index," then click OK.

Step 10—FrontPage lets you preview your work by selecting the Preview Tab at the bottom of the page. You can also preview the page using your computer's browser. To do this, go to the File menu and select Preview In Browser. Your browser window will open with your new page displayed.

The next step in building the web site will be to define the gallery system and create the individual gallery pages—i.e. high fashion, wedding, commercial, and sports.

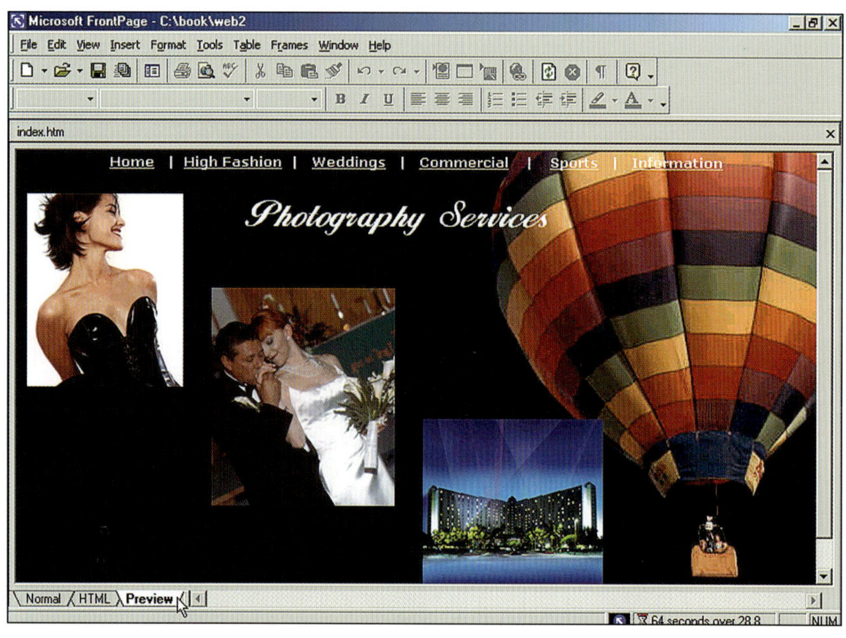

Figure 5-12: Preview window of Frontpage to see how your page will appear on the Internet.

DEFINING THE GALLERY PAGES

Frames. A photography studio that provides multiple services needs to demonstrate the capabilities of each of these services. To maintain a uniform appearance and make the gallery user friendly, this demonstration takes advantage of a frames-page system. This is a style of web page design in which the browser window is divided into discrete sections called frames. Each frame holds its own page, so a two-frame page is actually displaying two separate pages at the same time. You will see that this type of gallery provides the viewer with total control over a number of options with very few mouse clicks. First, let's examine how the system works and then check out the details of putting it all together.

In Figure 5-13, there are two frames making up the page. The first frame is on the left and displays the menu page; the second frame is on the right and holds the gallery page. The system will display four galleries (i.e. high fashion, weddings, sports, and commercial). The viewer makes a single mouse click to change galleries. Each gallery includes four thumbnails that can be clicked to show an enlargement, as seen in Figure 5-14. Additional selections may be added to the menu and several more pictures will fit into each gallery, so you are not limited to the selections shown here.

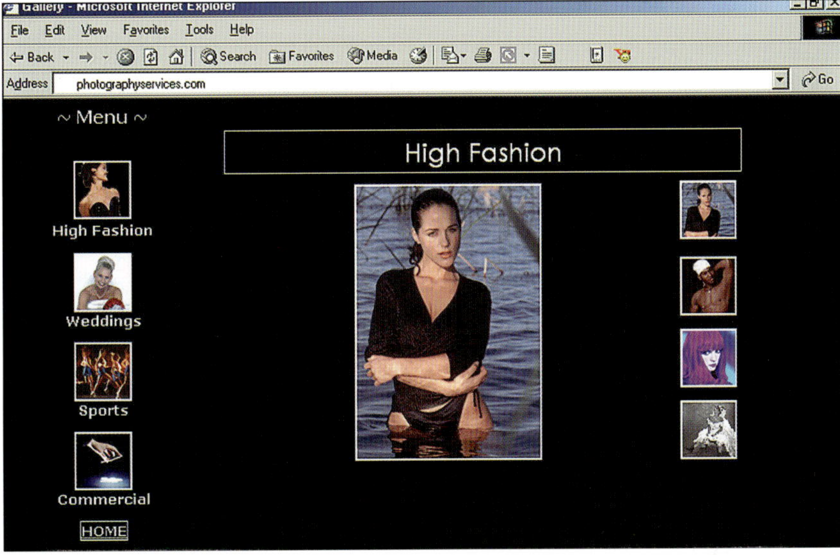

Figure 5-13: The gallery system using a frame page. Large photo by J.R. Sterling.

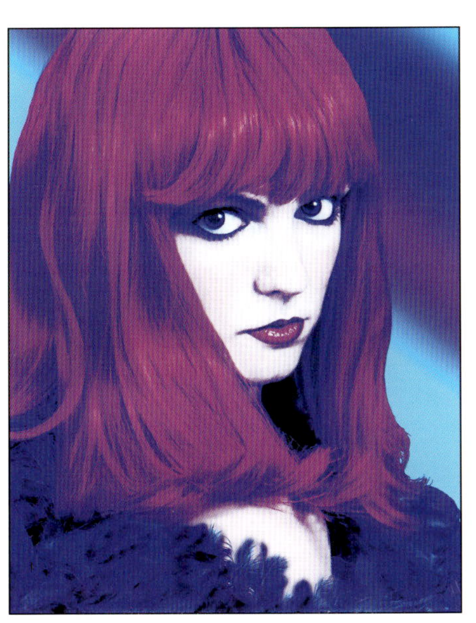

Photography by Deborah Lynn Ferro.

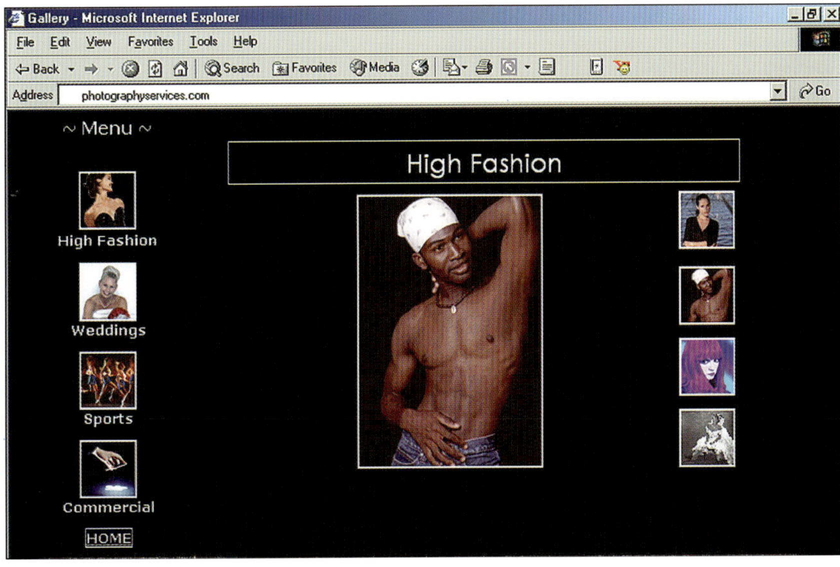

Figure 5-14: Clicking the next thumbnail in the gallery shows the enlarged photo. Large photo by J.R. Sterling.

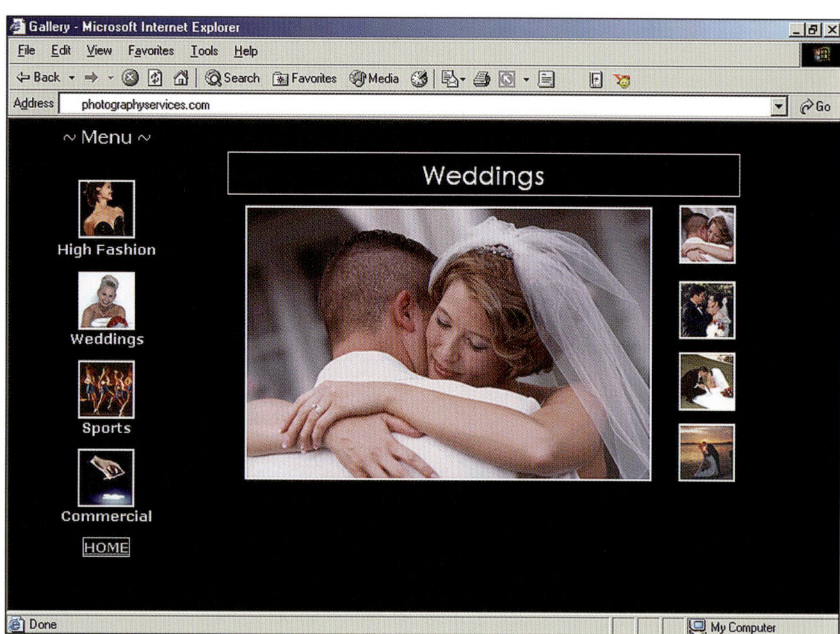

Figure 5-15: The wedding gallery is displayed in the gallery frame when selected from the menu. Large photo by Gary Fox.

Clicking on the "wedding" button in the menu frame displays the wedding gallery in the gallery frame. Notice that the menu is not affected when changing from one gallery to another.

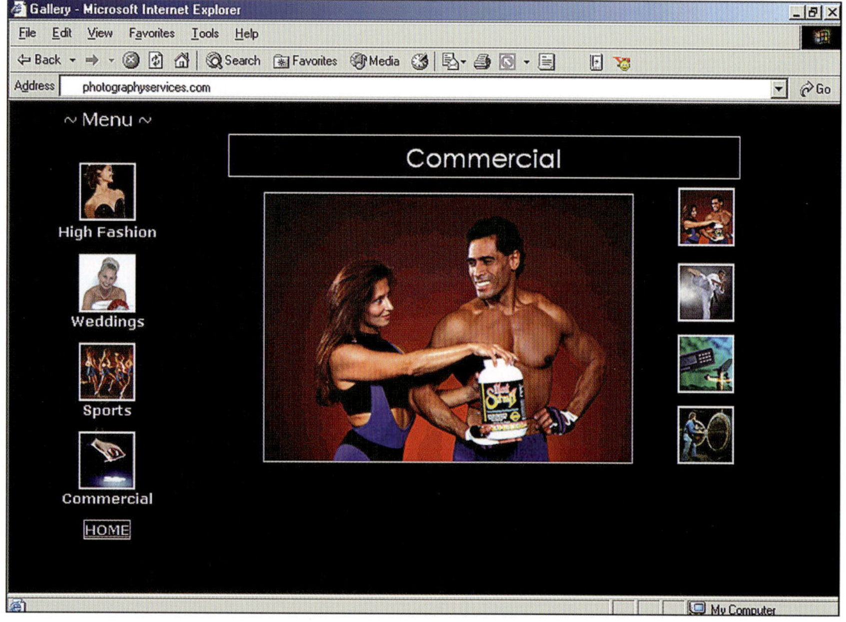

Figure 5-16: The commercial gallery called from the menu frame appears in the gallery frame. Large photo by Richard Cyril Coad.

Likewise, clicking on the "commercial" button in the menu frame displays the commercial gallery, and the "sports" button shows the sports gallery. The gallery frame is called the target of the menu frame, meaning a page called from the menu is displayed in the gallery frame.

Load Time. The menu frame is unchanged during the whole process. Why is this advantageous? As a web designer you should always try to minimize the load time of the pages in your web site.

Keeping the menu frame unchanged means it is only downloaded one time to the viewer's browser. The viewer can use the menu to change pages in the gallery frame without reloading the menu with each selection.

Figure 5-17: The Sports gallery called from the menu frame is displayed in the target or gallery frame. Large photo by Wayne Ebinger.

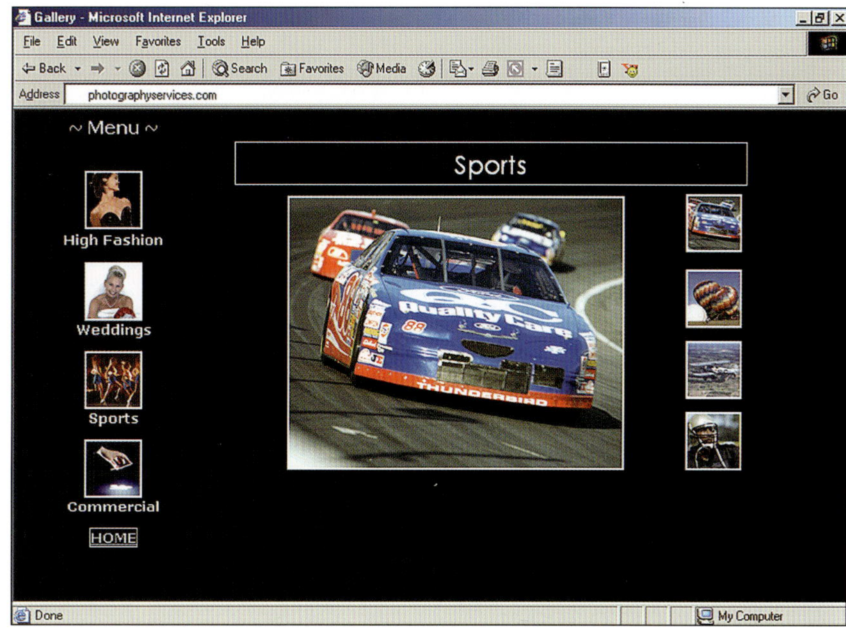

CREATING THE GALLERY

A diagram of the navigation system is shown in Figure 5-18. From the index page you can jump to any of the gallery pages by clicking on the appropriate gallery name in the menu bar. The initial page for each gallery is a frame page that shows the menu in the left frame and the first picture page in the right frame. In this diagram, the fashion gallery is enlarged for clarity. When requested by the viewer, the other picture pages are displayed in the gallery frame—shown as "fashion page 02", "fashion page 03", and "fashion page 04".

The complete gallery system consists of one menu page, sixteen gallery pages, and four frame pages. The gallery pages are the same except for the images displayed in them, so it will save time to make a gallery template. Once the gallery template is made you can insert the images for each gallery type and then re-save the individual updated pages with the appropriate new file names.

For this gallery type you need to plan and prepare your image and thumbnail sizes before you create your pages. In the demonstration, the thumbnail pictures are 54 pixels x 54 pixels. The maximum height of the display pictures is 254 pixels; the maximum width is 390 pixels. All pictures (whether a thumbnail or display) have a 2 pixel white frame prepared using Photoshop.

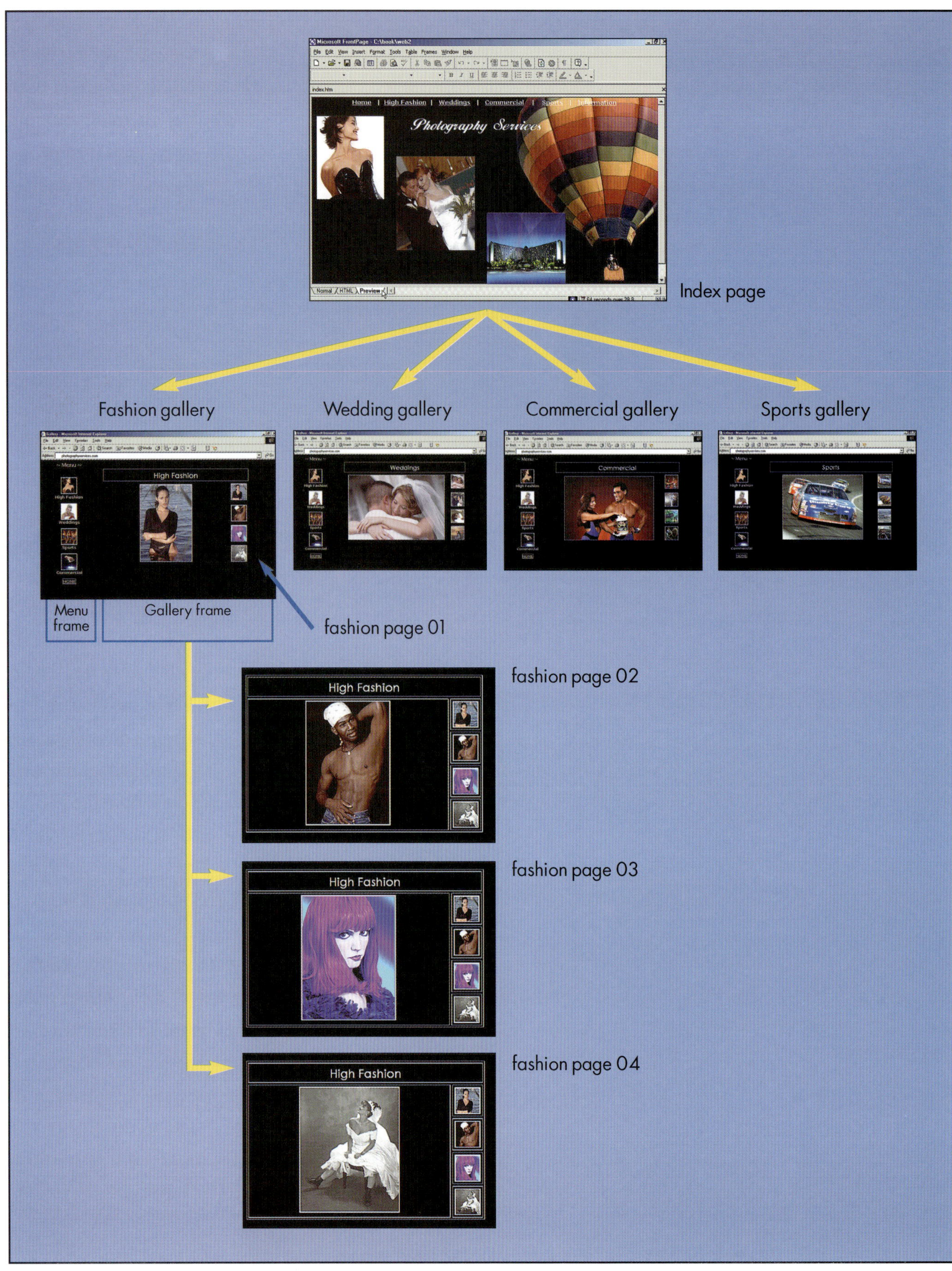

Figure 5-18: Navigation through the gallery system.

The Menu Page

Step 1—In FrontPage, open the web that you created at the beginning of this chapter. From the File menu select Open Web. In the dialog box, locate your web folder and click Open.

Step 2—To open a new page, go to the File menu and select New, and then choose Page. In the dialog box, select Normal Page and click OK.

Step 3—Next you need to title the page. To do this, right click on the page. In the pop-up menu, select Page Properties. Under the General tab, find the Title block and type the title of your page. Then click OK.

Step 4—From the Format menu, select Background. In the dialog box, set the background color to black and then click OK.

Step 5—From the Table menu select Insert and then choose Table. In the dialog box, set the parameters shown in Figure 5-19. Click OK. The table will be centered on the page.

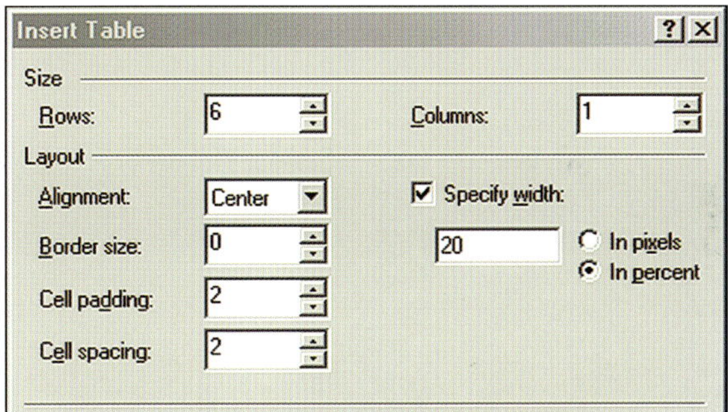

Figure: 5-19: The table properties window.

Step 6—Place you cursor in the top cell of the table. Select a font and font size and color. Click the Center Text icon from the toolbar. Type the word "~ MENU ~". To add a space below the word, hold down the Shift key and hit Enter.

Step 7—Place your cursor in the second table cell and click the Center Text icon.

Step 8—To place your first thumbnail picture in the cell, go to the Insert menu and select Picture and then select From File. In the dialog box, locate your picture file and click OK.

Step 9—Hold down the Shift key and hit Enter to move your cursor below the picture. Select the desired font, size and color, then type the description of your gallery. Continue this process in each cell until all of your galleries are listed. In the last cell type the word "HOME." This will be the link back to your front page. Your finished page should look like Figure 5-20.

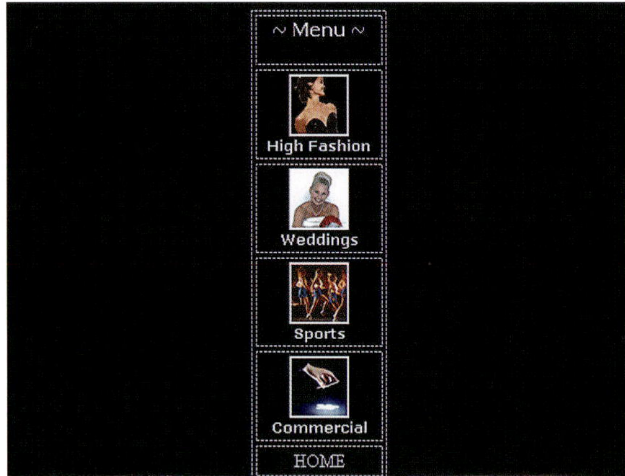

Figure 5-20: The completed menu page.

Step 10—Save the page. From the File menu select Save As. In the dialog box, name the page "menu" and click OK. This page will be used later in the frame pages and will be called by the name "menu.htm".

The Gallery Template

In this segment you will create the gallery page template. Once the template is made you will add the pictures for each gallery to make the gallery pages.

Step 1—From the File menu select New, and then choose Page. In the dialog box, select Normal Page and click OK.

Step 2—Right click on the page. In the pop-up menu, select Page Properties. Under the General tab find the Title block and type the title of your page and then click OK.

Step 3—To set the background color, go to the Format menu and select Background. Under Colors in the dialog box, set the background color to black and then click OK.

Step 4–Calculate the width for your table. Find the width of your largest display picture and add it to the width of your thumbnail pictures. In this example, the widest display picture is 390 pixels and the thumbnail is 54 pixels for a sum of 444 pixels. The table is set for 500 pixels—it's better to be a few pixels too large than to be too small.

Step 5—From the Table menu select Insert and then choose Table. In the dialog box, set the parameters shown in Figure 5-21. Click OK. The table will be centered on the page.

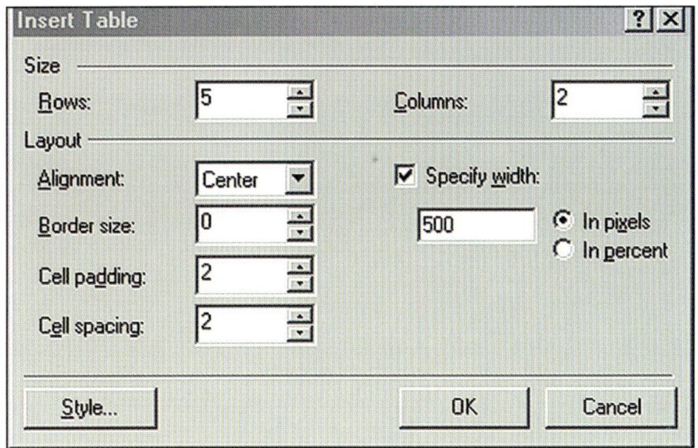

Figure 5-21: The gallery table settings.

Step 6—Next, we need to create the title cell by merging the two cells in the top row to form the title bar for the gallery. To do this, highlight the two cells, right click in the cell, and select Merge Cells from the pop-up menu.

Step 7—Right click in the resulting merged cell and select Cell Properties from the pop-up menu. In the Cell Properties dialog box, check the Specify Width box and set the cell width the same as the table width (500 pixels). Set the horizontal alignment to center.

Step 8—In the Cell Properties dialog box, click the Style button (located at the bottom of the box). Then click the Format button and select Border from the pull-down menu. Set the Style to solid, set the Color to white and the Border Size to 1 pixel. Click OK three times to exit these dialog boxes and apply the changes. When you have completed steps 7 and 8, the top cell should span the entire table and have a narrow white border.

Step 9—Next, merge the remaining cells in the left column. To do this, highlight the four cells, then right click inside the cells and select Merge Cells from the pop-up menu (Figure 5-22).

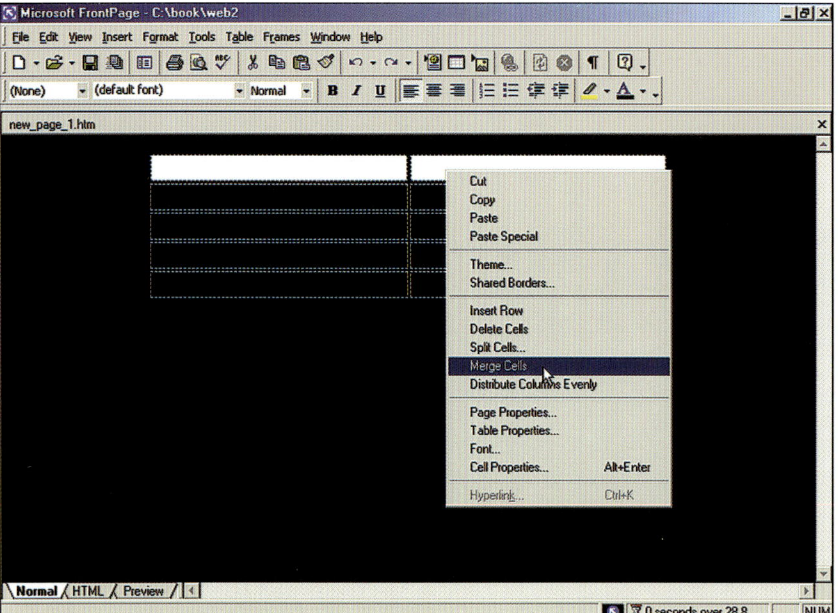

Figure 5-22: Merge the title cells.

Step 10—Right click inside the resulting cell and choose Cell Properties from the pop-up menu. In the Cell Properties dialog box, set the Horizontal Alignment to Center. To estimate the cell width setting, subtract the thumbnail width from the table width. For this example, the thumbnail width is 54 pixels and the table width is 500 pixels. Therefore, this cell will be set to 445 pixels wide (500–54=446). See Figure 5-23. Check the Specify Width box and insert your cell width in pixels, then click OK.

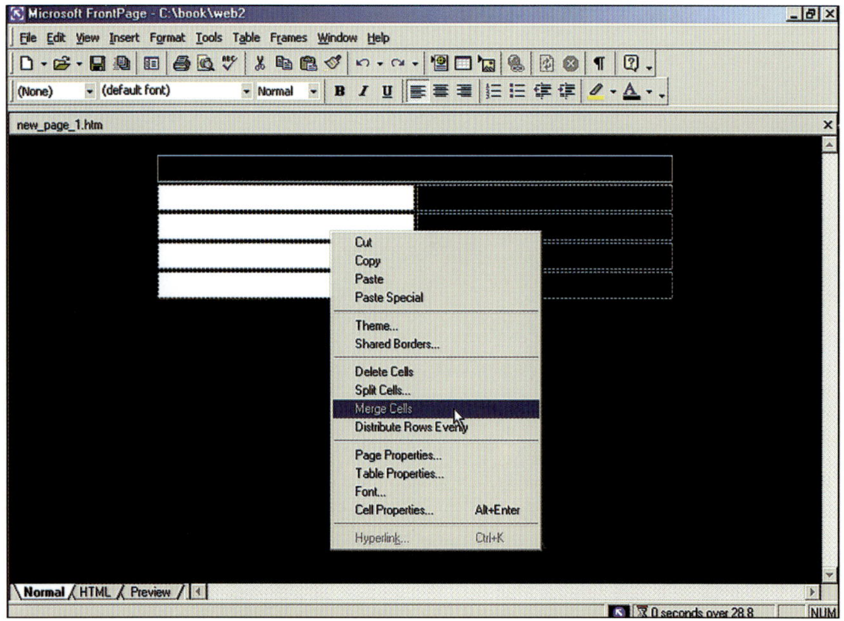

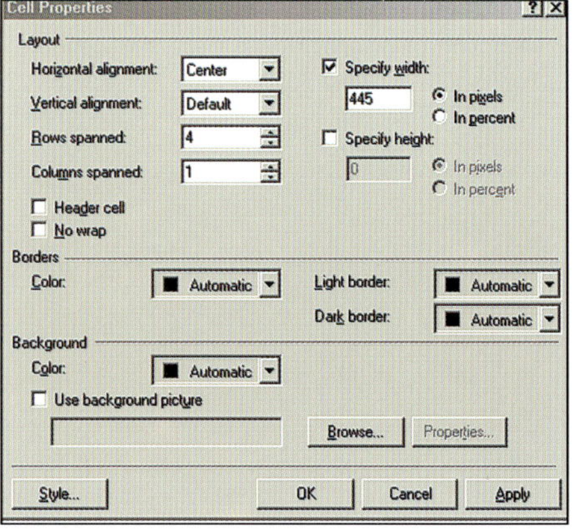

Figure 5-23 (left and above): Merge cells and set the cell properties for the picture display cell.

Step 11—Next, we'll create the thumbnail cells. To do this, highlight the remaining cells in the right-hand column. Right click and select Cell Properties from the pop-up menu. In the Cell

Properties dialog box, set the Horizontal Alignment to Center. Set the Cell Width to 55 pixels, set the Cell Height to 55 pixels. Remember, the thumbnails for this example are 54 pixels square and need to fit into these cells. Click OK. The resulting table will look like Figure 5-24. This completes the template!

Step 12—From the File menu select Save As and name the file "template".

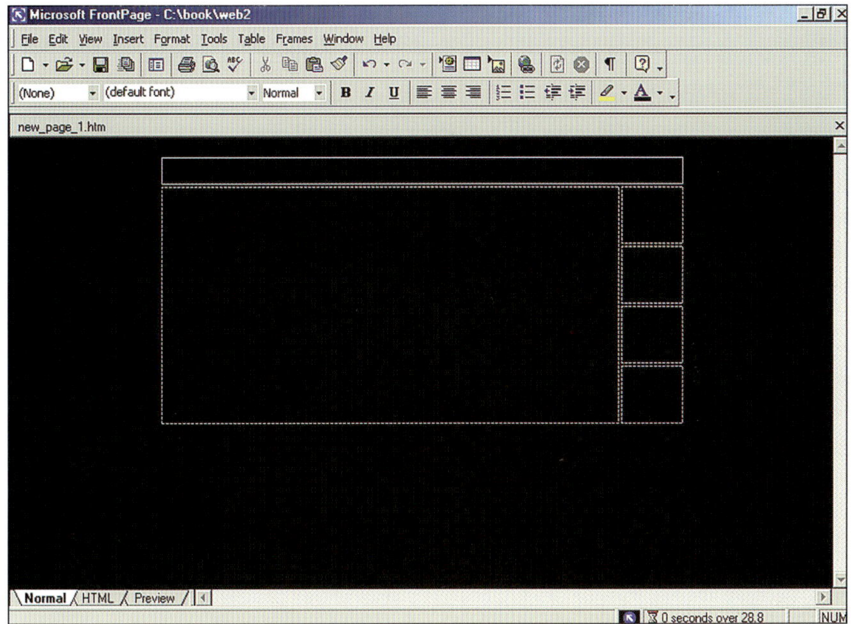

Figure 5-24: The final gallery template page.

Create the Gallery Pages

This demonstration gallery has sixteen gallery pages to be made from the template. There are four types of photography being displayed and four images per gallery. Assembling the pages is quite easy using the following technique.

Step 1—Open the "template" page. Place your cursor in the title cell. Choose a font, font size, and font color. Type the title of your first gallery. In this example the title is "High Fashion."

Step 2—Next insert the thumbnail pictures into the thumbnail cells. To do this, place your cursor in the top thumbnail cell, from the Insert menu select Picture and then select From File. In the dialog box, highlight the first thumbnail file for this gallery and then click OK. Repeat these steps for each thumbnail cell of your table. In this example, there are four cells.

Step 3—To finish this gallery page, insert the first display image in the display cell. To do this, place your cursor in the display cell of the table. From the Insert menu select Picture and then select From File. In the dialog box, highlight the large image file that corresponds to the first thumbnail image. Click OK. This completes the first page of the fashion gallery.

To finish this gallery page, insert the first display image in the display cell.

Step 4—From the File menu select Save As. In the dialog box you will notice that the page is already named "template". Highlight the name "template" in the File Name block, and then type the new name for the page. In this example, the new name is "fashion01".

Step 5—The remaining fashion gallery pages are simple to complete. You simply replace the display image from the page "fashion01" with the second display image, then save the updated page as "fashion02".

Here's how to do it. You should already have the "fashion01" page open. Right click on the large display image, and select Cut from the pop-up menu. The image disappears. From the Insert menu select Picture and then select From File. In the dialog box, highlight the large image file that corresponds to the second thumbnail image. Click OK. This completes the second page of the fashion gallery.

To save the page, go to the File menu and select Save As. In the dialog box you will notice that the page is already named "fashion01". Highlight the name "fashion01" in the File Name block, then type the new name for the page. In this example, the new name is "fashion02".

Step 6—Repeat step 5 until you have one page for each thumbnail image of your gallery. In this example there are four pages (shown in Figure 5-18) and named:

- fashion01.htm
- fashion02.htm
- fashion03.htm
- fashion04.htm

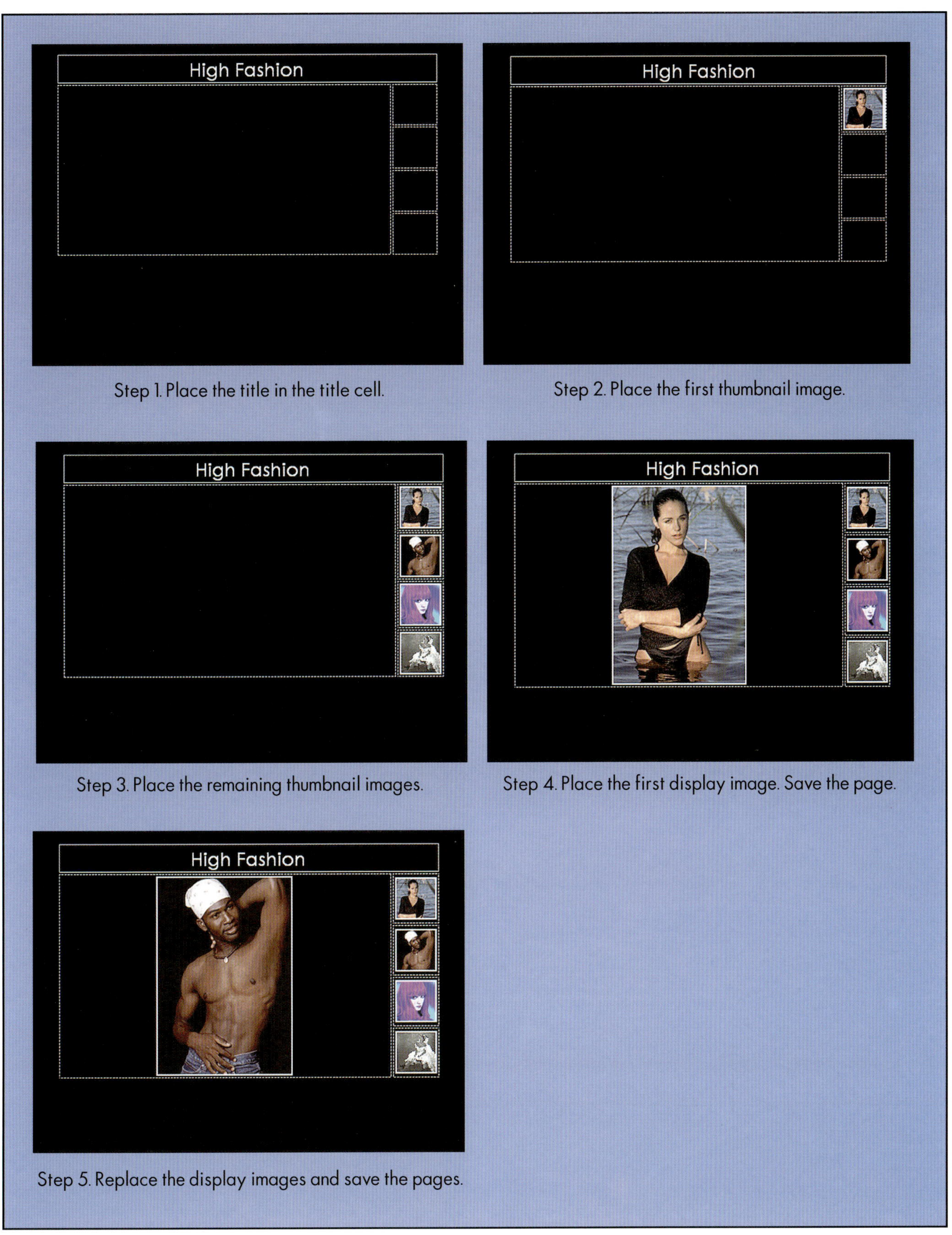

Figure 5-25: The steps involved in making the gallery pages.

Step 7—Next, we need to hyperlink the thumbnails so that, when clicked, they call up the correct enlargement. Begin by opening the page "fashion01.htm". Right click on the top thumbnail picture. In the pop-up menu select Hyperlink Properties. In the dialog box, highlight the page that contains the enlargement of the thumbnail. In this case it is "fashion01.htm". Click OK.

Step 8—Right click on the next thumbnail picture, and create a hyperlink to the page that contains the enlargement of the thumbnail ("fashion02.htm"). Repeat until you have created hyperlinks for each thumbnail image.

Step 9—Save the page.

Step 10—Repeat steps 7 and 8 for every gallery page (i.e. "fashion01.htm", "fashion02.htm", "fashion03.htm", and "fashion04.htm").

Now that you have completed the pages for the first gallery it will be easier to make the other galleries. Open the template page once again. Repeat the steps that you just completed for the fashion gallery except use the images from your other galleries. Save your pages with unique names to make it easy to identify them. In this example the pages for each gallery are as follows:

Now that you have completed the pages for the first gallery it will be easier to make the other galleries.

High Fashion	Weddings	Sports	Commercial
fashion01.htm	wedding01.htm	sports01.htm	commercial01.htm
fashion02.htm	wedding02.htm	sports02.htm	commercial02.htm
fashion03.htm	wedding03.htm	sports03.htm	commercial03.htm
fashion04.htm	wedding04.htm	sports04.htm	commercial04.htm

In addition to these pages, the "menu.htm" page will be used in the next section to complete the gallery system.

Create the Frame Pages

In this section you will create a frame page for each gallery. As part of the frame page layout you will link the buttons on the menu page (see page 91) to the galleries (see page 95).

Step 1—From the File menu select New, and then choose Page. In the dialog box, select the Frames Pages tab. In the dialog box, click on the Contents icon and then click OK.

Editing view—View where design guides that will be invisible in the final web page (such as the dotted delineating lines around tables) are visible for editing.

Step 2—The page that opens in the FrontPage editing view is divided into two sections. Look at Figure 5-26 for an explanation of the several features of this view. Each frame offers two options for filling the frame. If you have created the pages beforehand (which you have done in this example), you will choose Set Initial Page for each frame. The alternative is to build a new page within each frame in this frame view.

Step 3—Click on the Set Initial Page button in the left frame. In the dialog box, locate the file named "menu.htm". Highlight the file and then click OK. The menu page will appear in the left frame. It will probably not be aligned correctly at this time, but you will correct the alignment after the other frame is filled.

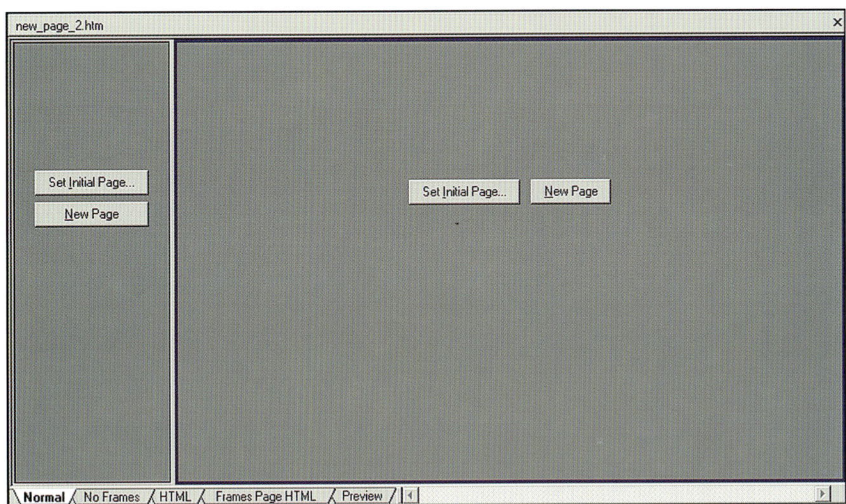

Figure 5-26: The frame page editing view before the frames are filled with pages. Each frame can be filled with a pre-existing page by selecting Set Initial Page, or a new page can be created by selecting New Page.

Step 4—Click on the Set Initial Page button in the right frame. In the dialog box, locate the file named "fashion01.htm" (see page 96). Highlight the file and then click OK. The first fashion

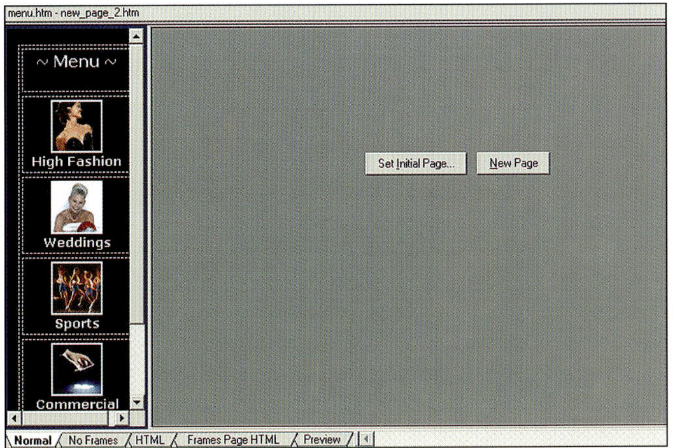

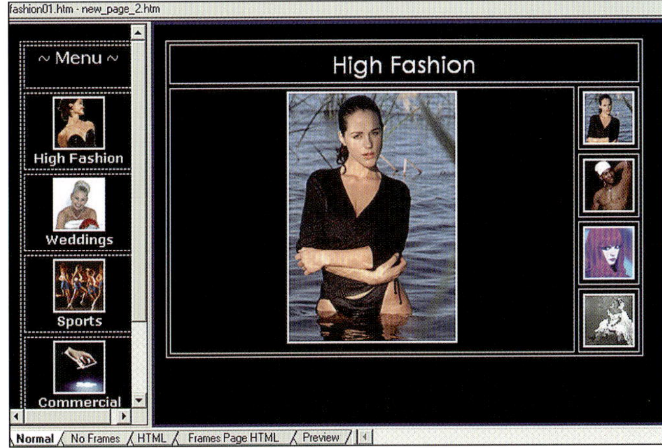

Figure 5-27: The preexisting pages "menu.htm" and "fashion1.htm" fill the left and right frames respectively.

gallery page will appear in the right frame. Your FrontPage editing window should look like Figure 5-27 after the first and second frames are filled with pages.

Step 5—Right click in one of the frames. In the pop-up menu, select Frame Properties. In the dialog box, click on the Frames Page button. In the resulting window, uncheck the Show Borders box. Click on the General tab and give your page a title in the Title block. Click OK to exit the General section, then click OK again to exit the Frame Properties dialog box.

Step 6—Now, we need to correct the frame border alignment so that the menu is completely visible. To do this, place your cursor on the vertical line that divides the two frames. A double-arrow icon will appear. Click the mouse and hold while you drag the line to the right; release the mouse button to set the line at its new position.

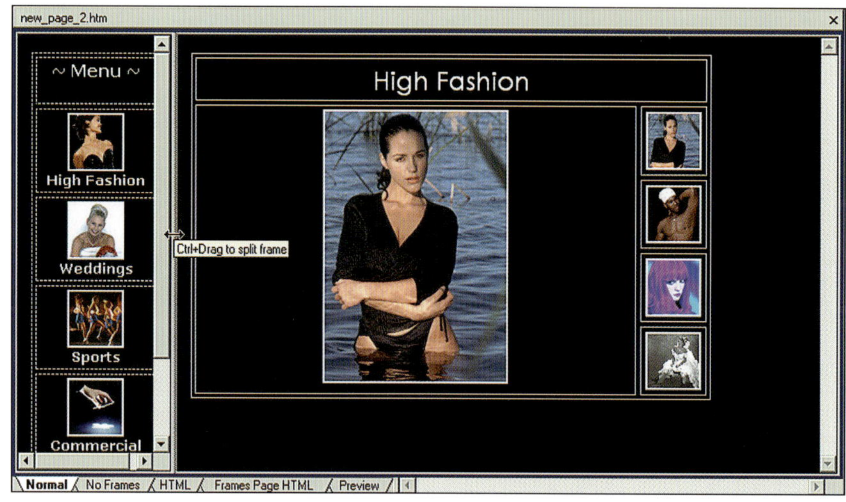

Figure 5-28: To reposition the frame divider, click on the border and drag it to its new location.

Step 7—From the File menu select Save As. In the dialog box, locate the blank page named "fashion.htm" that you created when you set up your home page menu. Click on Save. In the dialog box that asks if you want to replace the existing page click Yes. (If you did not create a blank page as suggested on page 79, you can name your page "fashion.htm" now. You will then need to go back to the home page and link this page to the menu [see page 91].)

Step 8—To create the other gallery frame pages, right click in the right-hand frame. In the pop-up menu select Frame Properties.

In the dialog box, go to the Initial Page block. Replace the page that is listed in this block with the first page of the next gallery. For instance, the page showing in the block now is "fashion01.htm". The next gallery is Weddings, so type "wedding01.htm" in the Initial Page block—or use the Browse button to locate the file and then click OK. Notice that the wedding gallery is now in the right-hand frame.

Step 9—Save the page as before, replacing the original blank page "wedding.htm" (see page 79), or naming the page wedding.htm.

Step 10—Repeat steps 8–9 for each of the galleries. For this example there are four framed-gallery pages named "fashion.htm", "wedding.htm", "sports.htm", and "commercial.htm".

Link the Gallery Pages

It's time to tie together all of the pages that you have created. Use the following steps to accomplish this.

Step 1—Open the page "fashion.htm". In the menu frame, right click on the thumbnail picture for the High Fashion gallery. In the pop-up menu, select Hyperlink Properties. In the dialog box, select the file "fashion01.htm" and then click OK. Now, when the viewer clicks on this thumbnail, the High Fashion gallery will appear in the right-hand frame.

It's time to tie together all of the pages that you have created.

Step 2—Right click on the thumbnail that represents the Wedding gallery and create the hyperlink to the "wedding01.htm" page. Repeat the process for the Sports gallery and Commercial gallery.

Step 3—Highlight the word "HOME". Right click and select Hyperlink Properties from the pop-up menu. In the dialog box, select the file "index.htm". Locate the Target Frame options box and select Parent Frame. Click OK. When the viewer clicks on the word "HOME", the first page of your web site will now replace the entire gallery page.

The gallery is now complete. Preview your gallery in the browser and test the hyperlinks from one gallery to the next and also test the

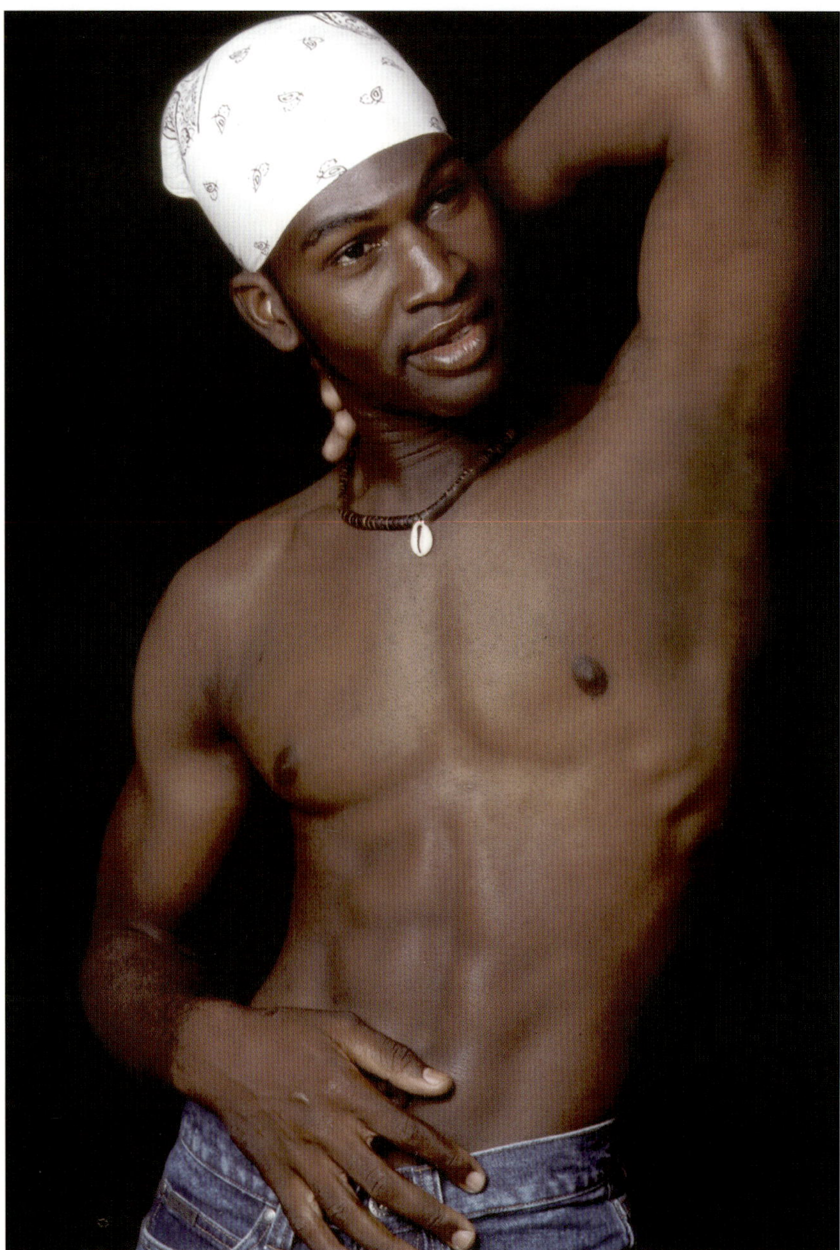

Photograph by J.R. Sterling.

hyperlinks that change pictures. Be sure to test the "HOME" button, and verify that the home page does not show up inside one of the frames.

► THE INFORMATION RESPONSE/REPLY FORM

In this section you will be creating your response/reply form (i.e. the information request page). This is the one page on which it is not necessary for you to include your complete menu. We do not even suggest adding a "home page button" on the form, because we want the client to immediately complete all fields before leaving the page. Using the browser's back button allows the user to leave the form page without leaving your web site.

To have an interactive page requires two steps:

1. Design your form page.
2. Configure your form so that you receive the information after your viewer has submitted it. Contact your hosting company for instructions.

If you are developing your web site using FrontPage software, it's a real plus to have FrontPage extensions installed on your site. When you're making a response/reply form using FrontPage and using a server that provides these FrontPage extensions, you will be able to set up your form so that the results are automatically e-mailed directly to you.

Extensions—Smaller software applications that add functionality to a larger application and are accessed from within that application (in this case, FrontPage).

Other Microsoft extensions will allow you to access information from other Microsoft software such as Excel, or to access informational databases. These are advanced topics that are covered in Microsoft manuals. Study the many capabilities of FrontPage extensions in your user's guide. This includes information on forms and form submissions.

Design the Form Page

Step 1—From the File menu, select New, and then choose Page. In the dialog box, select Normal Page and then click OK.

Step 2—Right click on the page; from the pop-up menu choose Page Properties. In the Page Properties dialog box, select the General tab and give your page a title. Select the Background tab and set your background color and/or background picture as you like. Click OK.

Step 3—Click on the Center button to center your text. Type a name for your page and instructions to your viewers. Hit your Enter key once to add a line (see Figure 5-29).

Step 4—From the Insert menu, select Form then choose Form. You will notice that a dotted box with a Submit button and a Reset button has now been added to your page.

Step 5—From the Table menu, select Insert and then choose Table. In the dialog box choose two columns and six rows (add

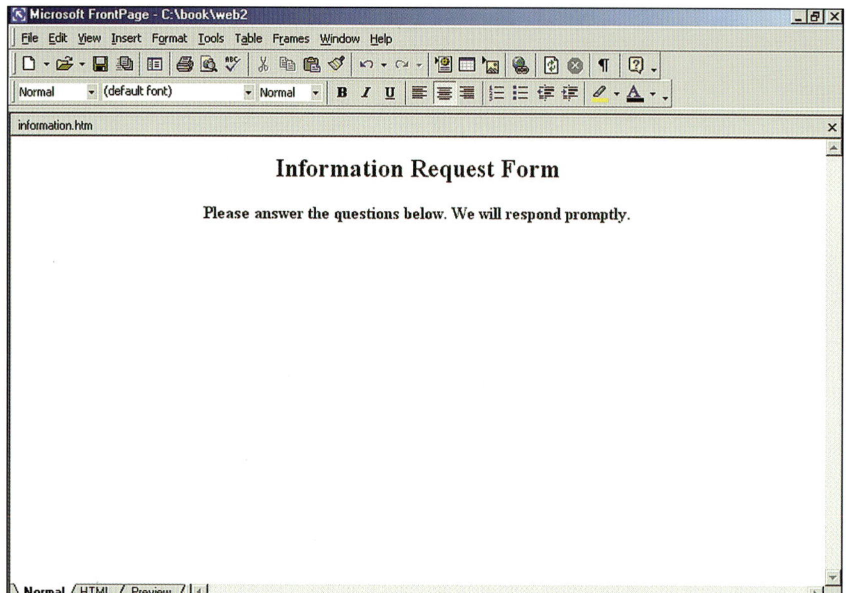

Figure 5-29: Centered title and text for the information reply form.

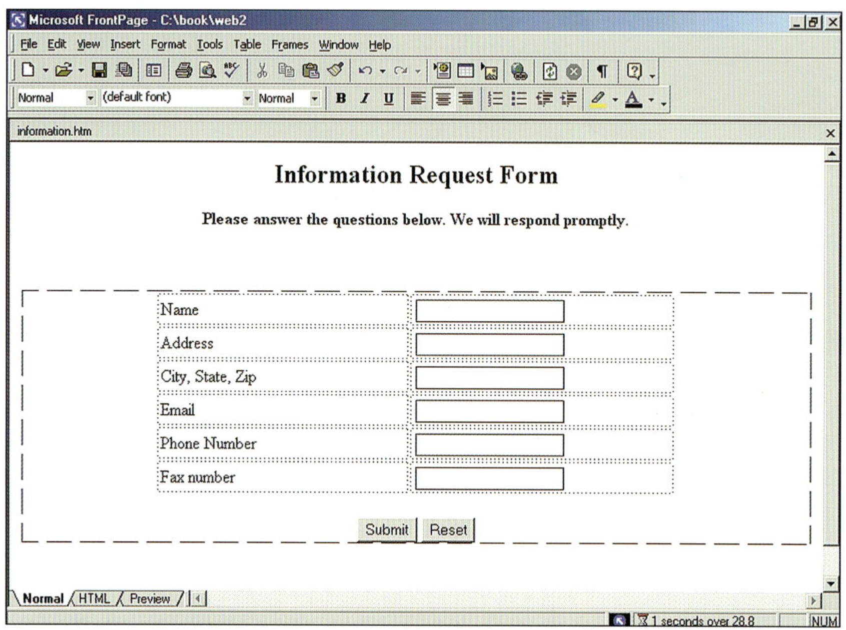

Figure 5-30: The form and form table are inserted in the page. The questions are typed in the lefthand column and the form boxes are located in the righthand column.

more rows to your table size if you have more than six questions). Choose a table width of 500 pixels, then hit OK.

Step 6—Type the categories of data to be entered by the visitor (or questions to be answered) in the left hand column. You might start with "Name", for example. Each question will then have a corresponding block directly to the right for the viewer to fill in the answer.

Step 7—Place your cursor in the cell to the right of the "Name" query. From the Insert menu, select Form and then choose One-Line Text Box. A box will appear in the table cell.

Step 8—Right click on the box. In the pop-up menu select Form Field Properties. In the dialog box, give the new text box a name that will associate it with the appropriate question. For example, the box adjacent to the "Name"query can be named "name". Your box names must begin with a letter, they cannot contain spaces. You can, however, use underscores to separate words (i.e. city_state_zip). You can give your box an initial bit of text by typing it in the Initial Value block. Most information forms do not use the Initial Value option. Set your character width to 20 (or to an appropriate number for the answer you expect to have input—i.e., a phone number block could be set at 15 characters). Click OK. Continue adding a one-line text box for the remaining questions.

Step 9—From the File menu select, Save As. Name the page "Information". If you have already saved a blank page named Information, then replace the blank with this page.

Further instructions are available for the use of other form options (using radio buttons, drop-down menus, check boxes, and scrolling text for example). With these basics in mind, you can refer to your Microsoft FrontPage user's guide for complete instructions on those specialized options.

Add the E-Mail Function

You may be able to set up the e-mail function of the form now.

If your site is hosted on a Microsoft Windows server, you may be able to set up the e-mail function of the form now. If this is the case, follow these steps:

Step 1—Right click on the form. In the pop-up menu, select Form Properties. In the dialog box, make sure the radio button for Send To is selected. Remove any information from the File Name block, and type your e-mail address in the E-mail Address block. Click OK.

Step 2—Save your page.

Once the form is complete, you can test it from the Internet. Open your form page on-line. Fill in the information blocks, and click Submit. If your form is working properly, you will receive an e-mail with the information that you supplied. If your form does not work, you will need to contact your hosting company for support. Request instructions for receiving form responses via e-mail.

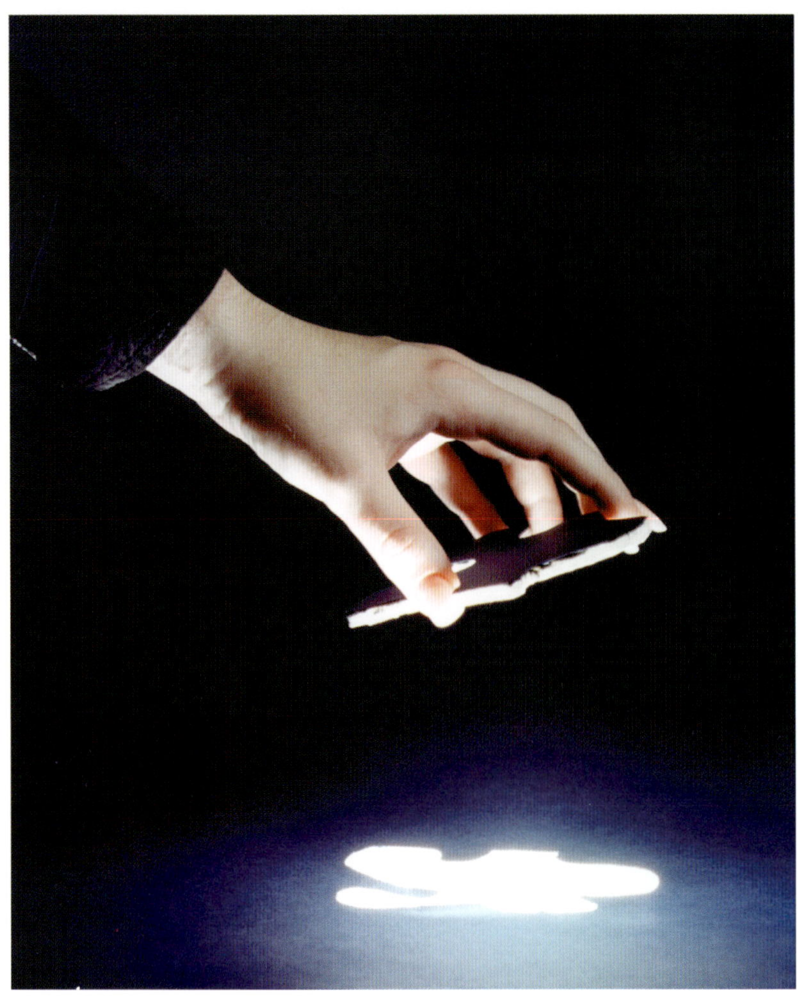

Photography by Robert Tancott.

▶ THE FINAL STEP

Congratulations! You have completed building your web site. You now have a home page named "index.htm". You have your gallery pages and your information form.

The final step is to preview your web site in your browser, check all of the links from page to page, and ensure that your images are properly placed. In FrontPage open your home page (index.htm). From the File menu select Preview in Browser. When your page opens in the browser; check all of your links; move from page to page. Test your gallery menu and thumbnail links. Test your e-mail link to be sure it opens your e-mail software with your correct e-mail address preinserted in the Send To box.

If your web site functions the way you intend it to, then you are ready to upload it from your hard drive to your hosting company's server.

If you are using FrontPage extensions and FrontPage software, follow these steps to upload your web site. From the File menu select Publish Web. In the dialog box, type your web address for your site (for example http://www.hollandrose.com), then click the Publish button. You'll be asked to provide a user name and password.

Otherwise, see chapter 7 for instructions on using FTP software to upload your site.

6. making the web work for you

WEB MASTER'S TOOLS

What does it mean to be a web master? Simply put, it means you control and maintain the various features of a web site. A web master performs the following functions:

1. Registers domain names
2. Obtains hosting services
3. Sets domain server addresses

Whether you are the web master for one site or several, you need to have a basic understanding of the above features, what they do and how to control them.

What does it mean to be a web master?

There are many companies that provide the services of registration and hosting, and each has their own specific method of interfacing with their clients. Most, however, provide you with a user name and a password that you will need in order to access your control pages.

Domain Name Registration. Domain name registration is accomplished by contacting a domain registrar, usually on-line. Many of these companies can be located by using the keywords "domain registration" in any search engine. You select a domain name that you want to use, then the domain registrar searches to determine if the name is available. If it is, you pay a yearly fee to register the name for your personal use. The domain registrar will provide a method of control for you, usually as a username and password and a control-panel web page.

Here are some helpful tips for selecting a domain name:

1. Choose a simple name that is easy to spell and easy to remember
2. If possible, include a word that describes your service (i.e., "smithphotography.com")
3. Do not use hyphens in your domain name (i.e., smith-photography.com)
4. If possible, select a ".com" name rather than ".cc" or ".net"

If your first choice for a domain name is not available, be careful about choosing the same domain name using ".net," ".cc," or using hyphens in your domain name. For example, suppose you want "smithphotography.com" as your domain name. It is not available, so you choose "smith-photography.com" or "smithphotography. net." Experience has shown us that people, by habit, will use the most common form of a domain name (in this case "smithphotography .com"), so choosing a less obvious form can cause confusion and send potential clients to a competitor's web site.

If your first choice is not available, be careful about using ".net," ".cc," or hyphens in your domain name.

Obtaining Hosting Services. Every web site is stored on a computer called a host or server. Companies that own and maintain host computers are called hosting companies. There are a number of companies who provide hosting services. These companies own and maintain computers that store your web site and allow visitors to view your web pages.

You should have a basic idea of how much memory space you will need for your web site. Hosting companies offer different plans with options like larger or smaller amounts of memory space, e-mail accounts, shopping carts and on-line credit-card processing. For a basic web site, you need about 200MB of memory and at least five e-mail accounts. Your host should be capable of processing on-line request forms into e-mails. Your host should provide around-the-clock technical support and they should back-up your web site in cases of power or computer failures.

Your hosting company will give you information on how to upload your web pages using file transfer protocol (FTP) software. Generally there are three items of information that you need to transfer your web site files:

1. FTP address
2. User name
3. Password

When you contract with a hosting company, they provide you with domain server addresses that tell Internet users where to locate your web site. It is the responsibility of the web master to record the domain server addresses with the domain registrar. Typical domain server addresses look like this:

NS10.VWH1.NET 209.238.9.50
NS11.VWH1.NET 209.238.9.51

Notice that there are two alphanumeric addresses with corresponding numbers. It is necessary to record these addresses with your Domain Registrar before your site will appear on the World Wide Web for viewers to see. The alphanumeric addresses are normally provided to you by e-mail once you contract with your host company.

Recording Domain Server Addresses with Your Registrar. To record your new domain server addresses, contact your domain registrar. Generally, you will go to your domain registrar's web site and select an option that allows you to manage your account. Typing your user name and password will then give you access to your registration information. Follow the instructions for changing your domain server addresses. Once your changes are made, it normally takes 24 to 48 hours for the change to take effect and for your site to show up on the World Wide Web. Then, when a user types your domain name (i.e., smithphotography.com), they will be directed to your host computer where they can view your web pages.

SEARCH ENGINES

A search engine is a web site that assists users in finding web pages that correspond to a particular topic. Every search engine uses three criteria to review placement for web sites: keywords, site titles, and site descriptions.

A search engine is a web site that assists users in finding web pages that correspond to a particular topic.

A keyword is a search word or phrase that is input by the user in order to find web sites that match the topic of the keyword. The search engine locates web sites that correspond to the keyword, it then displays the site title and site description of several sites. The user can decide which web sites to visit based on the descriptions provided. The search engine provides a hyperlink to the various sites for easy access.

When a user searches by keyword, the returned results of the search are ranked by the search engine. The ranking for your particular web site is determined by the search engine after visiting your site and scanning the title, keywords, and description. These three elements must be located in the source code of your web site using HTML tags. All three elements should be positioned inside the header of your page which will be described here.

Source Code—The source code of a web page is written in machine language for computers to translate into viewable web pages.

Title Tag. The HTML source code is made up of computer-language "tags" that appear before and after objects or text. A set of tags for the title of your site looks like this:

```
<title> your web site title </title>
```

Warning! Improper source code editing can damage the function and appearance of your web site. If you are not fully confidant of your abilities, you should consult a professional web master to make these changes.

In the example above, the opening tag is: <title>. The closing tag is: </title>. The text between the tags is the title of your web site. Try to be creative with the title of your site. Include what you do and where you are located. A Phoenix photography studio might use a title tag:

```
<title> Phoenix Arizona Photography: Rene's Portrait
Studio </title>
```

Keyword Tag. The tags for adding keywords and a description to your site are called meta tags. They are a bit different than the title tags and have the following general appearance.

Meta Tags—A portion of the HTML language that provide general information about the site to the various machines that are interpreting the HTML code (search engines, etc.).

```
<meta name="keywords" content="word, phrase,
word">
```

The words and phrases are enclosed in quotation marks and must be separated by commas. Select words and phrases that are relevant to your line of business. Use words that tell where you are located and what services you provide. Your keyword list should not exceed 250 characters. For example, a Phoenix, AZ, photography studio might use this keyword meta tag:

```
<meta name="keywords" content="Phoenix photog-
raphy, Arizona photographer, portrait, wedding">
```

When search engines visit your site, they are able to read these meta tags and store the keywords along with your site title and description in their database for future placement. When a user types one of your keywords as search criteria, the search engine will display your site in the list of matching sites.

Description Tag. The *description* meta tag is very similar to the *keyword* meta tag. The description meta tag has the following general appearance:

```
<meta name="description" content="A description
of your company goes here">
```

Write a description for your web site that will encourage the user to go to your site. The description must be enclosed in quotations and should not exceed 200 characters. Your description may contain several sentences. Some search engines will limit your description to fewer than 200 characters, so it is wise to put your most important words at the beginning of your description. Again, use as many keywords as possible in your description. Avoid statements like "the greatest photographer ever." Again, a Phoenix photography studio may use this description tag:

```
<meta name="description" content="Rene's Portrait
Studio serving the Phoenix, Arizona area for 25
years. Our professional staff will serve your portrait,
wedding, and commercial photographic needs.">
```

Header Tag. As mentioned above, the title, keyword, and description tags must be located in the header of your web page HTML source code. You must insert your tags into the source code using the HTML view of your editing software. First you need to locate the header of your web page. Near the top of the source code you will find an opening header tag that looks like this:

HTML view—A view of your web page where the HMTL code for the page (rather than the layout of the page) is displayed.

```
<head>
```

There will be information following this tag and then you will find the closing header tag that looks like this:

```
</head>
```

Insert your title, keyword, and description tags between the opening header tag and the closing header tag. Its often easiest to locate the closing tag </head> and simply add your lines of text above it. When you are finished, your code should be similar to this example (except there may be other lines of text in the header along with your tags).

```
<head>

<title> Phoenix Arizona Photography: Rene's Portrait
Studio </title>

<meta name="keywords" content="Phoenix photog-
raphy, Arizona photographer, portrait, wedding">

<meta name="description" content="Rene's Portrait
Studio serving the Phoenix, Arizona area for 25
years. Our professional staff will serve your por-
trait, wedding, and commercial photographic
needs.">

</head>
```

Your meta tags definitely need to be placed in the first page of your web site (index.htm). It's optional to put them on the other pages. You don't want the search engines to visit your web site before you have your title, keywords, and description tags in place so it's a good idea to put them on your page when the page is created before your site is submitted to search engines.

► SUBMIT YOUR WEB SITE TO THE SEARCH ENGINES

Some of the more popular search engines are listed on the facing page. Most search engines allow you to submit your web site to them for free. Each search engine has a different method for submitting your site, so giving explicit instructions here is impossible. You should go to each search engine home page and look for instructions for adding a URL, or submitting a site.

Most search engines allow you to submit your web site to them for free.

There are some free on-line services that allow you to add your site to several search engines at one time. Use the keywords "search engine submission" in any of the search engines and you will find a wealth of information. Software is also available that will automate your submission.

AltaVista.com	Infoseek.com
Excite.com	Lycos.com
Google.com	Webcrawler.com
HotBot.com	Yahoo.com

You may try changing your keywords, description and title to try to improve your search engine position.

We submit our sites no more than once a month. There are many new search engines and many new sites being submitted. You may try changing your keywords, description and title to try to improve your search engine position. It is time consuming and takes dedication to track your placement on all search engines.

7. updating your web site

FTP

The method discussed here for updating your web site may be accomplished using FTP software (File Transfer Protocol). This software allows you to make a connection from your home computer to your server through your Internet access line, pick the file that you want to transfer, and send the file to your server computer where it becomes part of your web site. The process of moving files to your server is called uploading. The process of moving files from your server (or the Internet) to your home computer is called downloading. It's as easy as moving a file from your hard drive to a floppy disk.

This software allows you to send the file to your server computer´ where it becomes part of your web site.

FTP software is available for purchase on line—you can type "FTP" in any search engine to locate a number of FTP software vendors. I use WS_FTP software however there are several capable products on the market. Once installed on your home computer, FTP software allows you to transfer files between your hard drive and a remote server—in this case, the computer where your web site resides for worldwide access.

Before accomplishing an FTP transfer, you will also need three pieces of information from your host company. These are as follows:

1. Your web site FTP address: ____________________
2. Your FTP user ID: ____________________
3. Your FTP password: ____________________

Generally, your web site FTP address is the same as your Internet web site address (your domain name). This information locates the server where your web site is stored. Your FTP user ID locates your web site on the server computer, and is assigned by your host company. Your FTP password is assigned by you (or your webmaster) to control access to your web site files.

UPDATING IMAGES

To replace an image, you need to know the dimensions and the name of the *existing image* that is currently shown on your web page. You should replace this existing image with one having the same dimensions. You want the size to be exact, so that you can avoid changing the layout of your web page. To determine the dimensions of the existing picture, follow the steps below:

Step 1—Open your web site on the Internet. Go to the page that contains the picture that you want to replace.

Step 2—Point at the picture and right click. In the drop-down menu, select Properties (Figure 6-1).

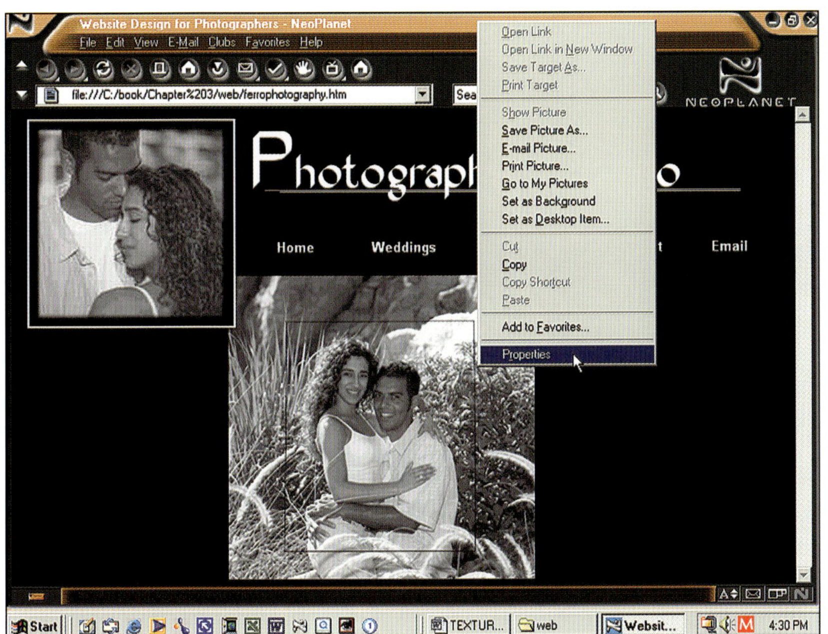

Figure 6-1: Getting the properties of a picture from the browser screen.

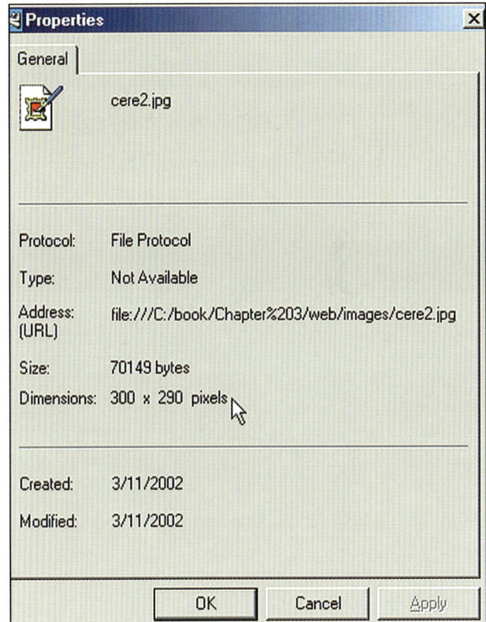

Figure 6-2: The picture properties box.

Step 3—The next pop-up window will display the name and dimensions of the picture (Figure 6-2). Record this information for use on your replacement photo.

Now that you know the name and dimensions of the photo on your web page you can prepare your replacement photo using

Photoshop or other image editing software. You need to name your replacement photo with the exact name and extension (.jpg or .gif) as the existing photo. In this example, the file name is cere2.jpg. Again, the size of the new image should also match that of the original that is being replaced. In this case, the new picture will need to be sized to 300 x 290 pixels and saved as cere2.jpg.

Uploading an Image. To upload your new photo file to your server follow these easy steps:

Step 1—Connect to the Internet using your Internet service provider (ISP).

Step 2—Open your FTP software and fill in the requested information for your web site. Figure 6-3 shows an example from the WS_FTP software. Yours may look different, but the required information is still the same. The Profile Name is whatever you want it to be. The Host Name/Address is your FTP address. Select Automatic detect for the HostType block. Fill in your User ID and Password, then click OK.

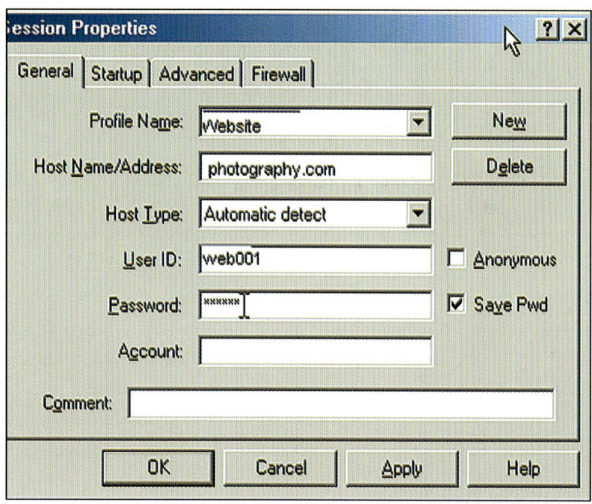

Figure 6-3: Logging into the FTP software.

Step 3—The next screen will open and will show the files from your host computer on the right and files from the hard drive of your home computer on the left. Your software (depending on the type you're using) may have a different appearance. You will, however, have access to your hard drive files and the files on your server (Figure 6-4).

Figure 6-4: The FTP software working window.

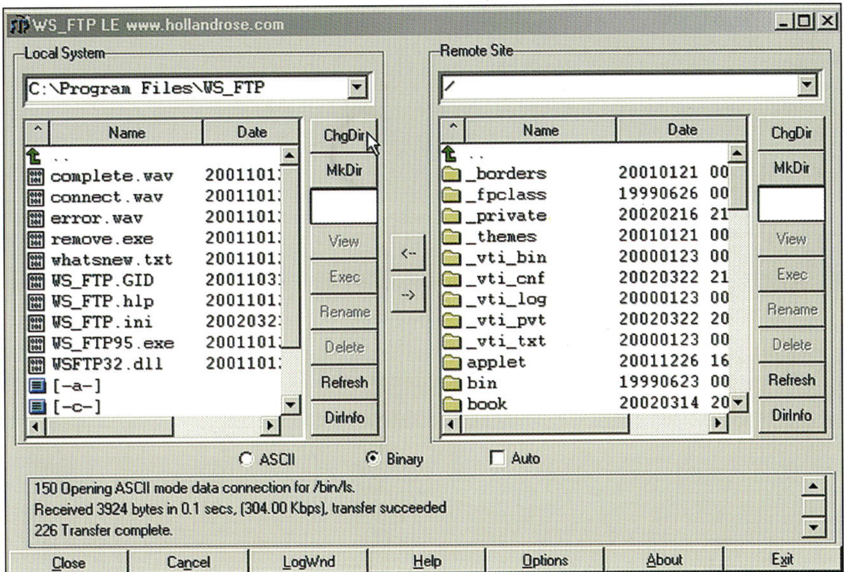

Step 4—On your hard-drive, locate the picture file that you want to transfer. Using the WS_FTP software, click on the Change Directory (ChgDir) button on the left side (your hard drive side). In the pop-up window, type the path to the folder holding your picture file (Figure 6-5).

Figure 6-5: Changing folders on the hard drive.

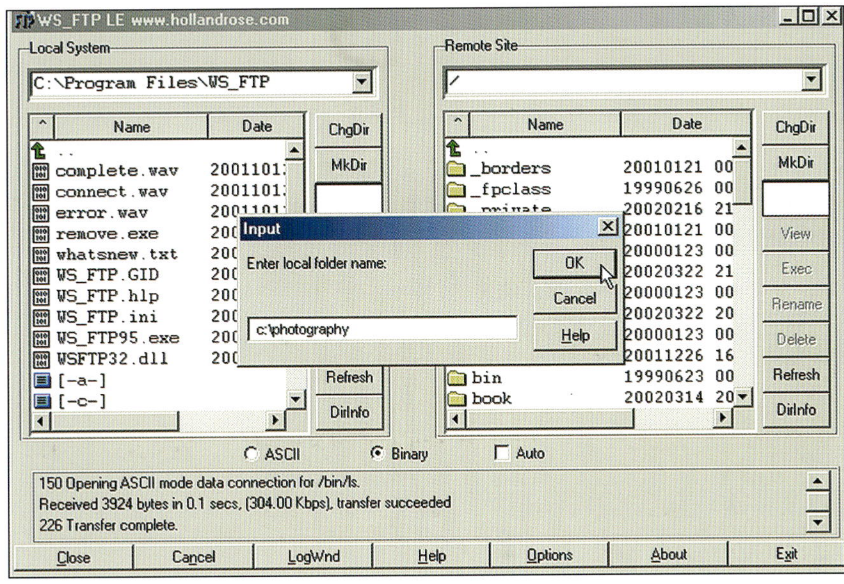

Step 5—Locate the old photo file that you are replacing. It will be in the right-hand window (among the host files), and should be named the same as your new photo. You may need to search through a few folders to find it. The filing system on the right-side window works just like Microsoft Explorer. In this example, cere2.jpg is replaced. Notice it is visible in both the left and right windows.

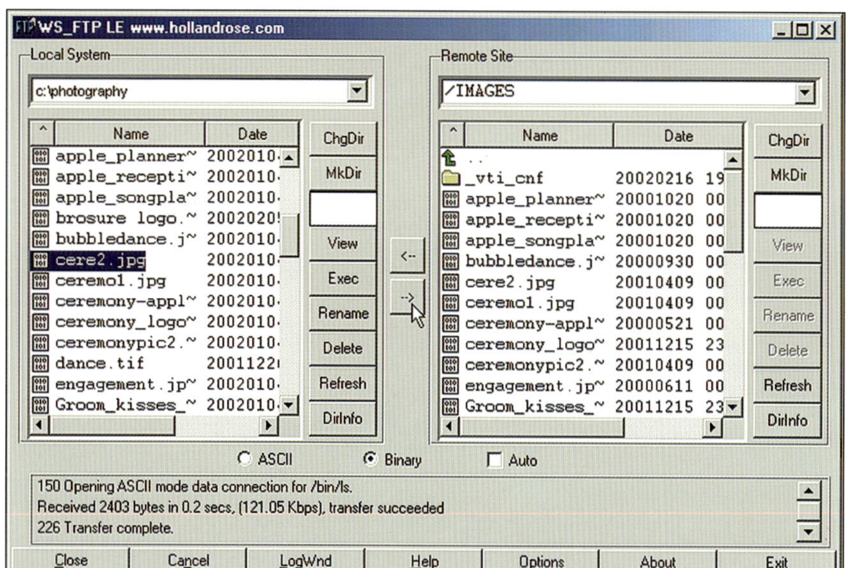

Figure 6-6: Moving a file from the hard drive to the server.

Step 6—Highlight the file to be transferred and click the arrow button that shows the direction of the transfer (Figure 6-6). That's it! Close your FTP software program.

You have now replaced the old image with a more recent one. Open your browser and check your page on the Internet to view the changes. You may need to "reload" or "refresh" your screen to get a new sample of your page downloaded from your server to your browser.

In closing, here are some helpful tips that can improve the look and feel of your web site, make it easy to navigate—and make it profitable for you and your studio!

DO

- Display your finest images and keep the number to a minimum
- Update your images regularly to feature new shots and replace outdated ones
- Make sure your meta tags are properly installed into the HTML code
- Include keywords and descriptive text for search engines on your home page
- Create a unique and catchy advertising slogan and use it throughout the site
- Include a response/reply form so customers can contact you easily
- Include a links page to boost your site's popularity
- Display your menu on every page (with the exception of the response/reply form) to make the site user-friendly
- Submit your site regularly to search engine databases

DO NOT

- Underline any text unless it is a hyperlink
- Use large fonts and loud colors to bring attention to text
- Choose loud flashy colors for the background of your web site

- Include disparaging remarks or put-downs about other photographers
- Display pricing information (create a "secret" address/page for this)
- Use long or numerous animations, slide shows or applets
- Use the word "contact"—this is too confrontational. Use "Information" or "About us" instead.
- Use the phrase "under construction." Search engines will log this and it will appear long after your site is completed and on databases world wide.

Karen Ault—Karen Ault assisted and was trained by her late husband, Wes Ault, of Aultamonte Photography Studio. They enjoyed many years of photographic success in central Florida as a top wedding team. Wes was loved and respected by all of his peers and he is truly missed. Karen still enjoys photographing when time permits, and we appreciate her photo contribution.

Richard Cyril Coad (*coadweddingphotography. com, Richardcoad.com)*—Richard is an Orlando-based commercial photographer, providing project versatility and proven excellence in photography since 1977 to clients in central Florida. His domestic and internationally published photography subjects include: industrial, real estate, small product, manufacturing/large product, food, lifestyle, architecture, architectural models, hotels/hospitality, packaging and executive portraiture. Richard's distinctive and unique style of wedding photography is also well known and admired. He was recently chosen by central Florida brides as the Wedding Professional of the Year in the photography category of "the knot's" *Weddingpages* magazine!

Wayne Ebinger *(Ebingerphotography.com)*—Wayne Ebinger is a versatile and talented wedding and sports photographer who served as the photographer for the Minnesota Twins Major League Baseball team and Alumni Association from 1977 to 1989. His photography has won an award from NMPA (National Motorsports Press Association) in 1999, and he has worked as a photographer for *NASCAR Winston Cup Scene* (NASCAR's number one trade publication) from 1989 to the present. Additionally, his wedding photography reflects blend of traditional and journalistic photography, with a nostalgic edge. Wayne's wife, "Bug," a photographer in her own right, adds a warm and unique approach to the Ebinger team.

Rick Ferro (*RickFerro.com)*—Rick Ferro is one of the nation's leading wedding photographers. In 1993, Walt Disney World approached Rick to create a wedding photography department. He became Senior Wedding Photographer for Disney—and Walt Disney World became the world's most sought after wedding destination! Rick also served as a photographer for ABC's *Weddings of a Lifetime* and for weddings on the highly successful *Regis & Kathy Lee Show*. He is the author of *Wedding Photography: Creative Techniques for Lighting and Posing*, and co-author of *Wedding Photography with Adobe Photoshop*, both published by Amherst Media. He also offers a speaking program, which he delivers to standing-room-only crowds at regional and national photography conventions. As a member of the Professional Photographers of America (PPA), Rick has earned his certification degree. His images have also been honored with inclusion in the Loan Collection and Showcase Collection. From Wedding and Portrait Photographer's International (WPPI), Rick holds a Master of Accolades degree. He has also been honored by Kodak with the Kodak Master Gallery Award.

Deborah Lynn Ferro (*RickFerro.com)*—Currently working toward her Master's degree in photography from Professional Photographers of America, Deborah educates other photographers considering digital technology. Deborah has extensive training in Photoshop, and is a member of National Association of Photoshop Professionals (NAPP). She is currently teaching a Photoshop class around the country called, "Practical Photoshop Techniques for Photographers." With her husband Rick Ferro, she is the co-author of *Wedding Photography with Adobe Photoshop*, published by Amherst Media. Their photography studio is called "Signature Studio" and is located in Jacksonville, FL.

Gary Fox (*GfoxFoto.com*)—Gary Fox has been documenting weddings for more than twenty years. He has developed a style of wedding photojournalism that tells a story and captures all of the emotion and special moments of the wedding day. His reputation as a top photojournalist is well known within the industry. Having a unique mastery of the art of photojournalism, artistic vision, and quick instincts, make him one of the most sought after wedding photojournalists on the east coast. Gary's images are greatly admired and aspired to. In his free time he enjoys instructing other photographers in this pursuit. His amazing images are a valuable contribution to our publication.

Wayne Lukens (*Lukensphotography.com*)—Wayne Lukens has been a wedding, portrait and aerial photographer for over twenty-five years. After completing course work toward his Ph.D in film/communications from the Clarmont Graduate School near Los Angeles, he moved to Miami to teach and to do public relations work for a small college. He became interested in wedding photography after photographing the daughter of his supervisor at the college. After several years of attending seminars and training, he opened his first photography studio in 1983. Since that time, has photographed over four thousand weddings. He was recently named Disney Photographer of the Year by the *Unofficial Disney Wedding Guide* for his work in wedding photography.

Rhett Pyle (*Artisticphotography.com*)—Rhett is a graduate of the Germain School of Photography, in New York City and worked as a manager for Bryn Alan Photography studios, in Miami, FL. In 1985, Rhett moved to Orlando and established his own business, Artistic Photography by Rhett Pyle. He and his wife, Wendy, specialize in weddings using natural-light photography, which softly conveys an added dimension to the photographs. Recognized by their peers for the ability to create outstanding wedding images, they are one of the top photography teams in central Florida. Long time members of WPPI, Rhett and Wendy's beautiful wedding-day images are featured in the slide show gallery.

Guillermo Rodriguez (*Guessphotography.com*)—Guillermo holds a degree in graphic arts and photography from the Technical Institute of Puerto Rico. Specializes in wedding, portrait, modeling and high fashion photography, Guillermo's Studio of Photography and Design (located in Orlando, FL) has gained such clients as The Hispanic Chamber of Commerce, *La Prensa* newspaper, and the Miss Puerto Rico of Orlando Pageant. He has served as the photographer for a number of very well known dog shows produced by Federacion Canofila de Puerto Rico and the American Kennel Club. His photographs have been published in magazines such as *Kennel Review* and *Dog World*.

Derek Smith (*Sunshinephotographics.com*)—The founder of Sunshine Photographics, Derek is a top central Florida wedding and commercial photographer. In 1990, Derek earned his BA in photography at Virginia Intermont College, one of the top ten photography programs in America. Derek is an advocate of digital photography and feels it allows him the freedom to become more creative during a photo shoot. Digital photography has allowed Derek to post images on line, which has increased his revenue.

J.R. Sterling (*SterlingPhotography.com*)—Bringing twenty years of photographic mastery to the wedding day, J.R. Sterling of Sterling Fine Art Photography, began his career in 1979 as a U.S. Navy photojournalist, gathering numerous awards for his courage as a member of the Beirut peace-keeping forces. He acquired his BFA from a prestigious school of visual arts, and an MFA from New York University. He worked as a fashion photographer for leading New York City modeling agencies, including Ford, Wilhelmina, and NOW. J.R. stands out in his ability to capture the character, emotions, and spirit of the individual—and the moment! His current images have been featured in *Orlando Leisure Magazine*.

Robert Tancott (*Southlightphotography.com*)—SouthLight Photography, Inc., has been operating in central Florida since 1993 and is one of the most sought-after and well respected commercial and wedding photography studios in the region. The owner, Bob Tancott, has over twenty-seven years of professional photography experience, including eight years doing photojournalism for newspapers and magazines. Bob is the current president of the Wedding Professionals of Central Florida, as well as a member of WPPI.

Actions—A set of steps that are saved as a single unit. This set can then be applied to enact that precise series of steps to single or multiple images.

Browser—A software program that allows you to connect with the World Wide Web (provided you have an Internet connection) and view the contents of web sites. Netscape Navigator and Microsoft Internet Explorer are currently two popular browsers.

Button—In web design, a button invites the user to click on it to move on to new information. The selection of shape, color and size depends on the individual use.

Cells—In a table, the small boxes defined by the horizontal and vertical lines.

DHTML (Dynamic Hypertext Markup Language)—Used to create dynamic effects based on user actions. For example, a dynamic menu can be created that will reveal hidden objects when the user points at the menu.

Editing view—View where design guides that will be invisible in the final web page (such as the dotted delineating lines around tables) are visible for editing.

Extensions—Smaller software applications that add functionality to a larger application and are accessed from within that application (in this case, FrontPage).

Filters—Built-in functions of Photoshop that the user can apply to enhance their images. There are four basic filter types. Filters that improve image quality, filters that add artistic effects, filters that add special effects and filters that perform technical corrections.

Frames—Devices used to divide a browser window into sections.

Front Page Editing View—The editing view allows the user to see the edits as they are made.

FTP(File Transfer Protocol)—This is the code that allows users to transfer files from one computer to another over phone lines. You transfer pages to your web site using FTP.

GIF (Graphics Interchange Format)—A file format for digital images.

Home page—The home page is the first page on a web site. That is, the page that comes up when you type in a URL and "go to" that site. Home pages usually contain general information about the site and have links to the other pages on the site.

HTML (HyperText Markup Language)—This is the programming language used by the World Wide Web. Just as PostScript allows users to produce desktop publishing documents with various fonts and graphics, HTML allows users to create documents for the Web.

HTML tags—Found in pairs, these are portions of the HTML language that define the type of information found between them. For example, the title of a web page starts with a title tag and ends with a title tag; the information between the two tags is the title itself.

HTML view—A view of your web page where the HMTL code for the page (rather than the layout of the page) is displayed.

HTTP (HyperText Transport Protocol)—The standard for moving hypertext files across the Internet.

Hyperlink—A hyperlink is an object (text or graphic) containing a link to a web page. When you click on a hyperlinked object, you are automatically connected with another web page. It might be another page on the same site, or it might be a page on a different site.

Java Applet—A computer application written in Java computer language. For web developers, these offer a wide range of styles and methods for displaying images and text. Java Applets may be purchased on-line and inserted into web pages to produce dynamic effects.

JavaScript—A computer scripting language that enables web authors to design interactive sites. Javascript can interact with HTML source code, enabling web authors to spice up their sites with dynamic content.

JPEG (Joint Photographic Expert Group)—A file format and method of data compression for digital images.

Meta tags—A portion of the HTML language that provide general information about the site to the various machines that are interpreting the HTML code (search engines, etc.).

Microsoft Extensions—Programs that reside on a server (computer). Some Microsoft-developed web sites use these extension programs to add dynamic features.

Mouse-over effects—A JavaScript element that triggers an item in a web page (usually a graphic) to change when the mouse passes over it. The change usually signifies that the item is a link to related or additional information. Mouse-overs are widely used in navigation bars, pop-up boxes, and/or form submissions.

MP3 sound files—MP3 is the file extension for "MPEG, audio layer 3". Layer 3 is one of three coding schemes (layer 1, layer 2 and layer 3) for the compression of audio signals. MP3 is a compression scheme for audio files, just as JPG is a compression scheme for image files. Because MP3 files are small, they can easily be transferred across the Internet.

Noise—An effect that allows you to add the digital equivalent of film grain to images.

Pop-up Window—A pop-up window is a separate and independent browser window in which enlarged images may be displayed. Enlarged images are displayed that correspond to thumbnail images.

Raster graphics—Images that are made up of dots or pixels of color (like a digital photograph). These have large file sizes that load slowly on the Internet. Contrast with vector graphics.

Search engine—A search engine is a web site that assists users in finding web pages that correspond to a particular topic.

Server—The software used by people with a home page to let you look at their stuff, or the computer on which it is held by a service provider.

Service provider—A service provider is a company that provides users with Internet access. For example, AOL (American Online) is a service provider—when you join, you get access to AOL services, access to the Internet, and (if you join at a certain rate) space on their server for a small web site. There are also companies that provide direct access to the Internet and allow you to set up larger web sites.

Source code—The source code of a web page is written in machine language for computers to translate into viewable web pages.

Streaming—A technique for transferring data such that it can be processed as a steady and continuous stream. Streaming technologies are becoming increasingly important with the growth of the Internet, because most users do not have fast enough access to download large multimedia files quickly. With streaming, the client's browser or plug-in can start displaying the data before the entire file has been transmitted.

Style sheet properties—In web design, a style sheet is a file that defines the layout properties of a web page. When you fill in a style sheet, you specify such parameters as the font, background, and color scheme that will remain consistent throughout the web site.

Table—A table is a rectangle divided into sections using vertical lines and horizontal lines. The small boxes defined by the horizontal and vertical lines are called "cells" The group of cells that stack horizontally are called "columns." The group of cells that align vertically are called "rows."

Thumbnail—A miniature display of an image that can be enlarged by clicking on it.

URL (Uniform Resource Locator)—Also known as an address, this is the string of characters you type into your browser to reach a certain web site. For example, http://www.scamwatch.com is the URL for the ScamWatch web site.

Vector graphics—Images made up of mathematically-calculated line, curve, color and position properties. These have small file sizes that load quickly on the Internet. Contrast with raster graphics.

WWW (World Wide Web)—The Web is a part of the Internet that allows users to view documents containing text, graphics and hyperlinked objects.

Other Books from

Amherst Media

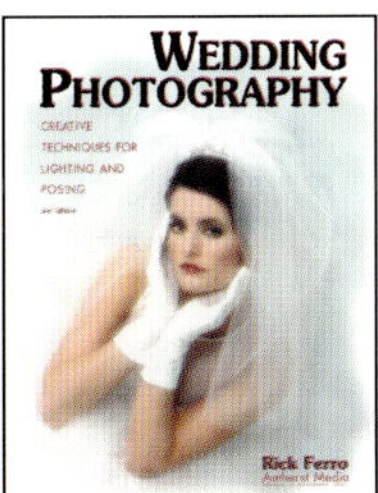

Wedding Photography

Creative Techniques for Lighting and Posing, *2nd Edition*

Rick Ferro

Creative techniques for lighting and posing wedding portraits that will set your work apart from the competition. Covers every phase of wedding photography. $29.95 list, 8½x11, 128p, full-color photos, index, order no. 1649.

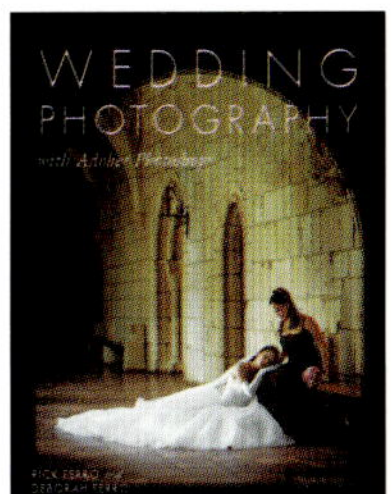

Wedding Photography with Abode Photoshop

Rick Ferro and Deborah Ferro

Learn how Photoshop can boost your creativity and your sales with this step-by-step guide. Packed with easy-to-learn techniques you can put to use right away to enhance your images and generate new business. $29.95 list, 8½x11, 128p, full-color photos, index, order no. 1754.

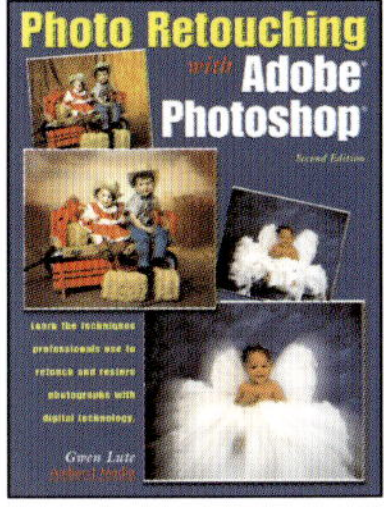

Photo Retouching with Adobe® Photoshop®

2nd Edition

Gwen Lute

Designed for photographers, this manual teaches every phase of the process, from scanning to final output. Learn to restore damaged photos, correct imperfections, create realistic composite images and correct for dazzling color. $29.95 list, 8½x11, 120p, 60+ photos, order no. 1660.

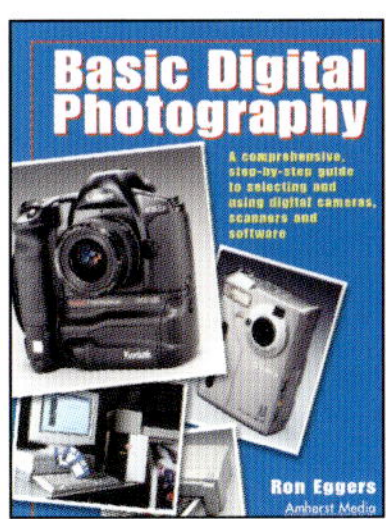

Basic Digital Photography

Ron Eggers

Step-by-step text and clear explanations teach you how to select and use all types of digital cameras. Learn all the basics with no-nonsense, easy to follow text designed to bring even true novices up to speed quickly and easily. $17.95 list, 8½x11, 80p, 40 b&w photos, order no. 1701.

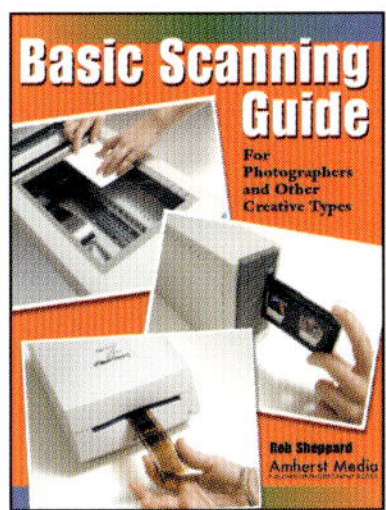

Basic Scanning Guide For Photographers and Other Creative Types

Rob Sheppard

This how-to manual is an easy-to-read, hands on workbook that offers practical knowledge of scanning. It also includes excellent sections on the mechanics of scanning and scanner selection. $17.95 list, 8½x11, 96p, 80 photos, order no. 1702.

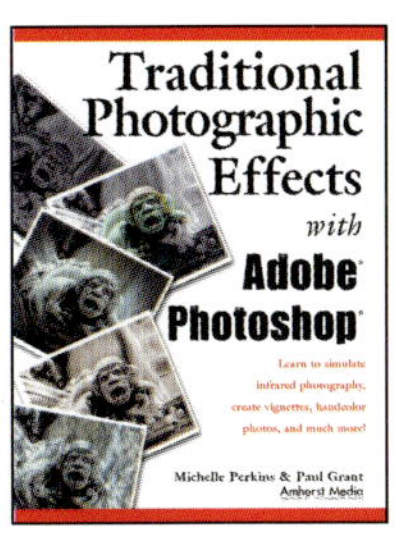

Traditional Photographic Effects with Adobe® Photoshop®

Michelle Perkins and Paul Grant

Use Photoshop to enhance your photos with handcoloring, vignettes, soft focus and much more. Every technique contains step-by-step instructions for easy learning. $29.95 list, 8½x11, 128p, 150 photos, order no. 1721.

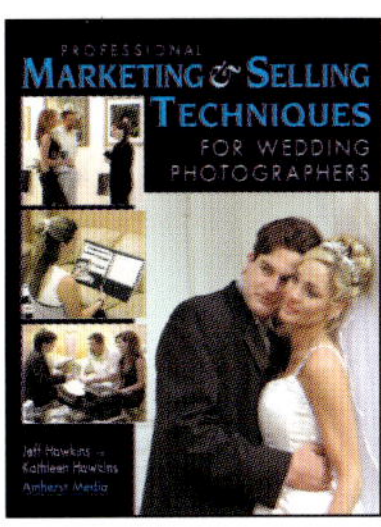

Professional Marketing & Selling Techniques for Wedding Photographers

Jeff Hawkins and Kathleen Hawkins

Learn the business of successful wedding photography. Includes consultations, direct mail, print advertising, internet marketing and much more. $29.95 list, 8½x11, 128p, 80 photos, order no. 1712.

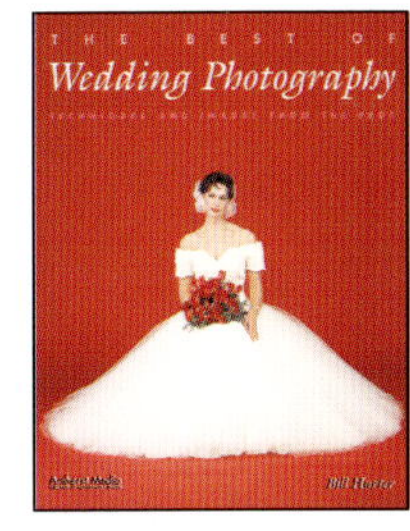

The Best of Wedding Photography

Bill Hurter

Learn how the top wedding photographers in the industry transform special moments into lasting romantic treasures with the posing, lighting, album design and customer service pointers found in this book. $29.95 list, 8½x11, 128p, 150 full-color photos, order no. 1747.

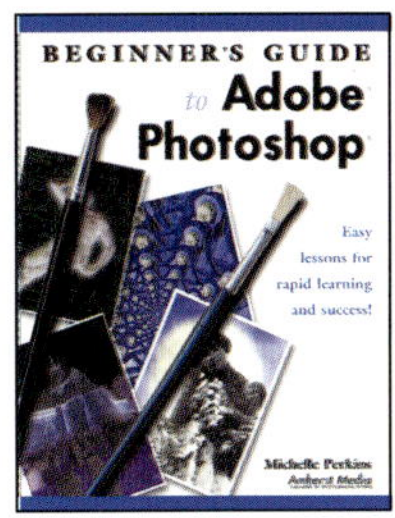

Beginner's Guide to Adobe® Photoshop®

Michelle Perkins

Learn the skills you need to effectively make your images look their best, create original artwork or add unique effects to almost any image. All topics are presented in short, easy-to-digest sections that will boost confidence and ensure outstanding images. $29.95 list, 8½x11, 128p, 150 full-color photos, order no. 1732.

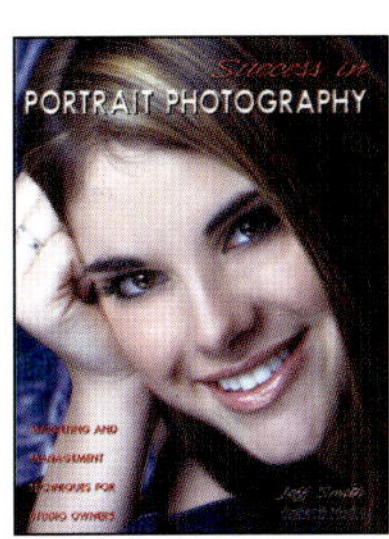

Success in Portrait Photography

Jeff Smith

No photographer goes into business expecting to fail, but many realize too late that camera skills alone do not ensure success. This book will teach photographers how to run savvy marketing campaigns, attract clients and provide top-notch customer service. $29.95 list, 8½x11, 128p, 100 full-color photos, order no. 1748.

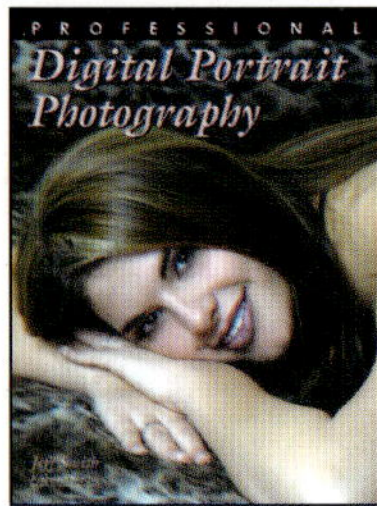

Professional Digital Portrait Photography

Jeff Smith

Digital portrait photography offers a number of advantages. Yet, because the learning curve is so steep, making the tradition to digital can be frustrating. Author Jeff Smith shows readers how to shoot, edit and retouch their images—while avoiding common pitfalls. $29.95 list, 8½x11, 128p, 100 full-color photos, order no. 1750.

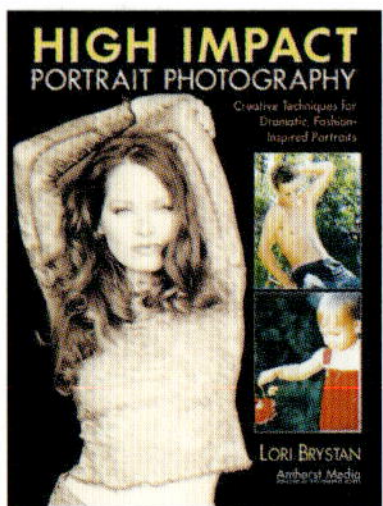

High Impact Portrait Photography

Lori Brystan

Learn how to create the high-end, fashion-inspired portraits your clients will love. Features posing, alternative processing and much more. $29.95 list, 8½x11, 128p, 60 full-color photos, order no. 1725.

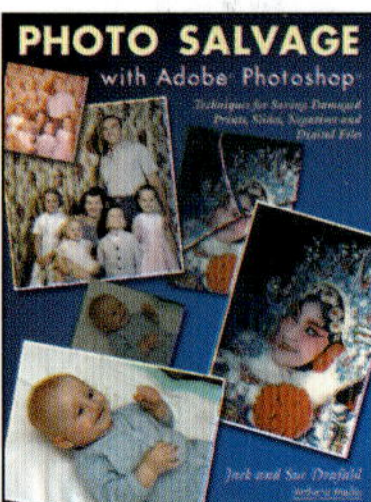

Photo Salvage with Adobe® Photoshop®

Jack and Sue Drafahl

This indispensible book will teach you how to digitally restore faded images, correct exposure and color balance problems and processing errors, eliminate scratches and much, much more. $29.95 list, 8½x11, 128p, 200 full-color photos, order no. 1751.

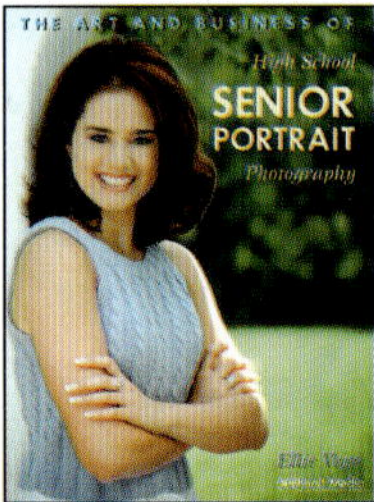

The Art and Business of High School Senior Portrait Photography

Ellie Vayo

Learn the techniques that have made Ellie Vayo's studio one of the most profitable senior portrait businesses in the United States. Covers advertising design, customer service skills, clothing selection, and more. $29.95 list, 8½x11, 128p, 100 full-color photos, order no. 1743.

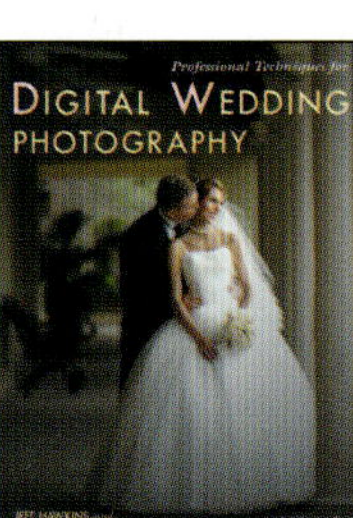

Professional Techniques for Digital Wedding Photography

Jeff Hawkins and Kathleen Hawkins

From selecting the right equipment to building an efficient digital workflow, this book teaches how to best make digital tools and marketing techniques work for you. $29.95 list, 8½x11, 128p, 80 full-color photos, order no. 1735.

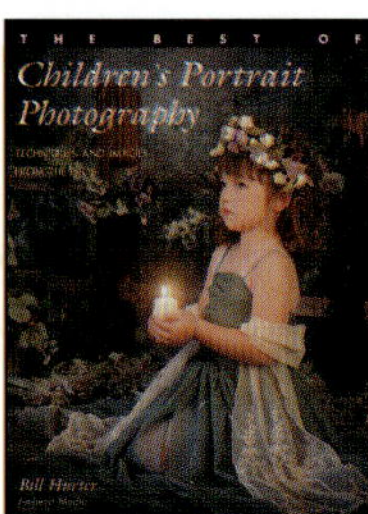

The Best of Children's Portrait Photography

Bill Hurter

See how award-winning photographers capture the magic of childhood. *Rangefinder* editor Bill Hurter draws upon the experience and work of top professional photographers, uncovering the creative and technical skills they use to create their magical portraits. $29.95 list, 8½x11, 128p, 150 full-color photos, order no. 1752.

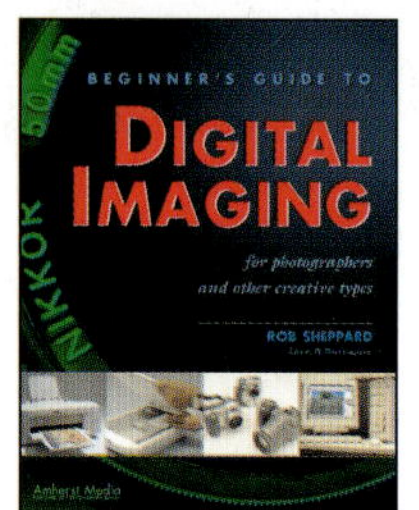

Beginner's Guide to Digital Imaging

Rob Sheppard

Learn how to select and use digital technologies that will lend excitement and provide increased control over your images—whether you prefer digital capture or film photography. $29.95 list, 8½x11, 128p, 80 full-color photos, order no. 1738.

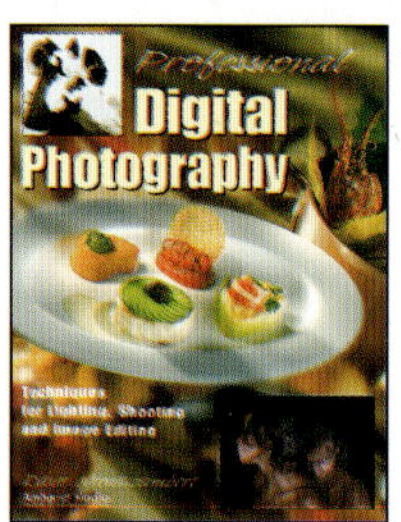

Professional Digital Photography

Dave Montizambert

From monitor calibration, to color balancing to creating advanced artistic effects, this book provides photographers skilled in basic digital imaging with the techniques they need to take their photography to the next level. $29.95 list, 8½x11, 128p, 120 full-color photos, order no. 1739.

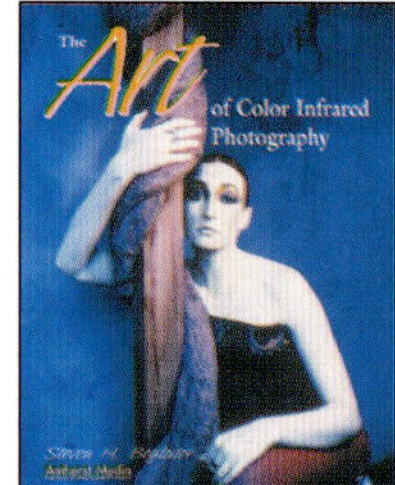

The Art of Color Infrared Photography

Steven H. Begleiter

Color infrared photography will open the doors to an entirely new and exciting photographic world. This exhaustive book shows readers how to previsualize the scene and get the results they want. $29.95 list, 8½x11, 128p, 80 full-color photos, order no. 1728.

More Photo Books Are Available

Contact us for a FREE catalog:

AMHERST MEDIA
PO BOX 586
AMHERST, NY 14226 USA

www.AmherstMedia.com

Ordering & Sales Information:

INDIVIDUALS: If possible, purchase books from an Amherst Media retailer. Write to us for the dealer nearest you. To order direct, send a check or money order with a note listing the books you want and your shipping address; Visa and MasterCard are also accepted. For domestic and international shipping rates, please visit our web site or contact us at the numbers listed below. New York State residents add 8% sales tax.

DEALERS, DISTRIBUTORS & COLLEGES: Write, call or fax to place orders. For price information, contact Amherst Media or an Amherst Media sales representative. Net 30 days.

1(800)622-3278 or (716)874-4450
FAX: (716)874-4508

All prices, publication dates, and specifications are subject to change without notice.

Prices are in U.S. dollars. Payment in U.S. funds only.